Grief and the Loss of
an Adult Child

The Foundation of Thanatology Series, Volume 8

Other Volumes in the Series

Grief and the Loss of an Adult Child

edited by

Otto S. Margolis
Austin H. Kutscher
Eric R. Marcus
Howard C. Raether
Vanderlyn R. Pine
Irene B. Seeland
Daniel J. Cherico

with the editorial assistance of
Lillian G. Kutscher

PRAEGER

New York
Westport, Connecticut
London

Library of Congress Cataloging-in-Publication Data

Grief and the loss of an adult child.

   (Foundation of Thanatology series ; v. 8)
   Bibliography: p.
   Includes index.
   1. Bereavement—Psychological aspects. 2. Adult
children—Death—Psychological aspects. 3. Parents—
Psychology. 4. Cancer—Patients—Family relationships.
5. Traffic accidents—Psychological aspects.
6. Death—Psychological aspects. I. Margolis, Otto
Schwarz. II. Series: Foundation of Thantology series
(Praeger Publishers) ; v. 8.
BF575.G7G73 1988   155.9'37   87-18315
ISBN 0-275-91304-X (alk. paper)

Library of Congress Catalog Card Number: 87-18315

ISBN: 0-275-91304-X

First published in 1988

Praeger Publishers, One Madison Avenue, New York, NY 10010
A division of Greenwood Press, Inc.

Printed in the United States of America

∞
The paper used in this book complies with the
Permanent Paper Standard issued by the National
Information Standards Organization (Z39.48-1984).

10 9 8 7 6 5 4 3 2 1

Thanatology is a discipline whose focus is on the practice of supportive physical and emotional care for those who are life-threatened, with an equal concern exhibited for the well-being of their family members. Proposed is a philosophy of caregiving that reinforces alternative ways of enhancing the quality of life, that introduces methods of intervention on behalf of the emotional status of all involved, that fosters a more mature understanding of the dying process and the problems of separation, loss, bereavement, and grief.

The editors wish to acknowledge the support and encouragement of the Foundation of Thanatology in the preparation of this book. All royalties from its sale are directly assigned to this not-for-profit, tax exempt, public, scientific, and educational foundation.

Contents

Part I

Grief and the Loss
of an Adult Child

1

The Family Under Stress: The Death of Adult Children

Stephen B. Shanfield, G.A.H. Benjamin, and Barbara J. Swain

The death of adult children is considered to be unnatural, yet it is a relatively frequent event. For instance, in the age range from 20 to 34, traffic accidents account for 34 percent of all deaths (U.S. Bureau of the Census 1985). Individuals who die in traffic accidents are usually young adults, and their parents are in the midlife age range (Shanfield and Swain 1984; Shanfield, Swain, and Benjamin 1986-1987). Similarly, cancer is the second leading cause of death and accounts for 21 percent of all deaths among those age 20 to 34 (U.S. Bureau of the Census 1985). However, the incidence increases with age, so that as a cause of parental bereavement, it is less common than traffic accidents. Most of those who die of cancer and whose parents are still living are in the midlife age range, and their parents are elderly (Shanfield, Benjamin, and Swain 1984). In spite of the frequency of parental bereavement, the literature on the loss of adult children is small. It has been studied under the specific circumstances of war (Purisman and Maoz 1977; Gay 1982) and a train wreck (Singh and Raphael 1981). This chapter describes parental bereavement resulting from the death of adult children in traffic accidents (Shanfield and Swain 1984) and as a result of cancer (Shanfield, Benjamin, and Swain 1984).

METHOD

Sixty-four bereaved parents were studied about two years after the death of their children. Forty parents whose children had died in traffic accidents were studied. The names of these individuals were obtained from their children's death certificates. There were 20 men and 20 women. Their mean age at the time of their children's death was 50.4 years. The average age of the children was 24.6 years at the time of death. About half of these children had died suddenly; the remainder died within hours to days after their accidents.

Twenty-four parents whose children had died of cancer were studied. The names of the parents were obtained from the records of individuals who had died at a hospice. The 8 men and 16 women in this group had an average age of 63.3 years at the time of their children's death. The average age of their children was 37.7 years at the time of death. The children who had died of cancer were ill for an average of about 35 months before death occurred. Both sets of parents completed a bereavement questionnaire. This questionnaire sought information about the parent and the child, other members of the family, and the relationships among them during three periods: (1) the year prior to the child's death; (2) the time around the death; and (3) the time between the death and the completion of the questionnaire. There were many similar items on the questionnaires given to both sets of parents, in addition to items assessing the responses to the specific type of death.

The parents of the accident victims filled out the Symptom Checklist 90 (SCL-90), which is a well-validated self-report survey measuring psychiatric distress along nine symptom dimensions and three global indexes (Derogatis 1979). The parents of the cancer victims completed the Brief Symptom Inventory (BSI), which uses 53 of the original 90 items of the SCL-90 and is scored along similar dimensions (Derogatis 1982). These have a very high correlation and can be compared with ease (Derogatis 1979).

RESULTS

The parents whose children had died in traffic accidents scored significantly higher on the SCL-90 symptom dimensions and global indexes than did a comparative normative population. In contrast, the mean BSI scores of the parents whose children had died of cancer were not different from those of a normative population.

Ninety percent of the accident parents were still grieving, in contrast to 70 percent of the cancer parents. The accident parents also experienced more guilt than the cancer parents. There was a significant increase in the number of health complaints among the accident parents, whereas the cancer parents reported no changes in their health.

The cancer parents experienced more frustration in the year before the death of their children. Eighty-seven percent of the cancer parents expressed some relief that their child had died. More relief was expressed by parents whose children had experienced longer illnesses.

Essentially, all of the parents in both groups still thought about their children. Seventy-five percent of the accident parents felt their children's presence, in contrast to 44 percent of the cancer parents.

There were many personal changes in the parents that occurred as a result of the death of the children. Many parents experienced a sense of personal growth on a number of dimensions, including an increased ability to discuss painful emotional issues. In addition, there were many changes in the families. Many parents felt closer to their spouses and other children.

Among the accident parents, mothers were more symptomatic than fathers. Among the cancer parents, mothers felt the loss to be more painful than fathers did.

In contrast to parents who lost children to protracted illness, parents whose children died suddenly were more symptomatic. If children were younger at the time of death, the parents experienced more distress.

Parents whose children died in single-car, single-driver accidents had higher levels of distress, depressive symptoms, grief, and health complaints. For the parents of accident victims, a dysfunctional family relationship characterized by frustration and anger before the death is a forerunner of increased guilt during the bereavement period. Among the parents of cancer victims, such relationships are associated with increased symptoms during the bereavement period.

DISCUSSION

The death of adult children as a result of traffic accidents and cancer produces a myriad of complex changes in their surviving parents. The parents continue to grieve, to think of their children, and to feel their presence. Many parents experience a sense of personal growth. The event is also a family event and produces changes in family structure over time. In some cases, the daily routine is markedly altered by changes in the habits and patterns of interaction built up over years, essentially the lifetime of the deceased child.

The sudden loss of adult children in traffic accidents, however, seems to produce a larger rent in the fabric of parents' lives. This group appears to be at risk for higher levels of psychiatric distress than expected. This is particularly so if their relationship with the dead child was ambivalent. They also experience more guilt and have more health complaints at the end of one year than do parents who have lost a child to cancer. Moreover, the accident parents are less expressive of their grief than the cancer parents. Parents who lose adult children to cancer do not have high rates of psychiatric distress, although they too undergo many changes. They appear less inhibited in their ability to express grief, which may be related to the finding that they generally do not have very many symptoms of psychiatric distress.

The nature of the relationship between parents and children changes over the life cycle, as does the character of grief. In

this sense, a family life cycle perspective is helpful in understanding the response to the loss (Fleck 1983). The relationship between young adult children and midlife parents is different from that between midlife children and their older
parents. Young adult children have not lived out their life
dreams and are more dependent on their parents. Indeed, the
accident parents appear to grieve for younger children more
intensely. These life cycle variables may also account for the
accident parents' increased levels of psychiatric distress. In
contrast, midlife adult children are less dependent on their
parents. They have their own lives and careers and have
lived out the main themes of their lives. These children usually
have their own children, who may be in their teenage years,
and have thus provided their parents with a sense of biologic
continuity. This may account for the finding of less psychiatric
distress among the cancer parents. These factors appear to be
important determinants of the character of the response to the
death of adult children.

One would ordinarily expect more frustration among
younger accident parents, whose children were struggling with
identity issues, than among cancer parents. The findings of
higher levels of frustration among bereaved cancer parents
was somewhat contrary to expectation. This finding is most
likely an effect of the illness. The cancer parents probably
experienced more frustration with their children in the year
before they died because of the length of the illness. This
conclusion is supported by the finding that parents whose
children experienced more protracted illness felt more relief
when their children died.

The different responses of mothers and fathers suggest
that a different relationship pertains between mothers and
their children. This merits further investigation. Increased
ambivalence in the relationship between parents and children
portends increased guilt for the accident parents and is associated with increased symptoms in the cancer parents. These
findings are similar to those obtained in studies of widows,
which have noted that problem relationships are forerunners
of difficulties in the bereavement period (Shanfield 1983).

The death of children in single-car, single-driver accidents
is predictive of increased psychiatric distress in parent survivors. Indeed, parents in this group appear to be at risk
for difficulties. Children who died in single-car, single-driver
vehicle accidents were also reported to have had more problems at the time of their death. This confirms previous studies
of this type of accident (Schmidt et al. 1972).

It is hoped that the data in this chapter will contribute to
the understanding of older families during the crisis of illness
and death (Shanas 1980). The death of adult children is a
relatively frequent event, yet remains a relatively unexplored
area of investigation. Further study on a prospective basis
is merited.

REFERENCES

Derogatis, L. 1979. *SCL-90 Norms.* Towson, MD: Clinical Psychometric Research.

————. 1982. *BSI Norms.* Towson, MD: Clinical Psychometric Research.

Fleck, S. 1983. "The Family: Past, Present, and Future." *American Journal of Social Psychiatry* 3: 25-38.

Gay, M. 1982. "The Adjustment of Parents to Wartime Bereavement." In N. A. Milgram, ed. *Stress and Anxiety,* vol. 8, p. 2437. New York: Hemisphere Publishing Co.

Purisman, R., and B. Maoz. 1977. "Adjustment and War Bereavement. Some Considerations." *British Journal of Medical Psychology* 50: 1-9.

Schmidt, C. W., S. Perlin, W. Townes, R. S. Fisher, and J. W. Shaffer. 1972. "Characteristics of Drivers Involved in Single-Car Accidents." *Archives of General Psychiatry* 27: 800-803.

Shanas, E. 1980. "Older People and Their Families: The New Pioneers." *Journal of Marriage and Family* 42: 9-15.

Shanfield, S. B. 1983. "Predicting Bereavement Outcome: Marital Factors." *Family Systems Medicine* 1: 20-26.

Shanfield, S. B., G. A. H. Benjamin, and B. J. Swain. 1984. "Parents' Reactions to the Death of an Adult Child from Cancer." *American Journal of Psychiatry* 141: 1092-1094.

Shanfield, B., B. J. Swain, and G. A. H. Benjamin. 1986-87. "Parents' Response to othe Death of Adult Children from Accidents and Cancer: A Comparison." *Omega* 17: 289-297.

Shanfield, S. B. and B. J. Swain. 1984. "Death of Adult Children in Traffic Accidents." *Journal of Nervous and Mental Disease* 172: 533-538.

Singh, B. and B. Raphael. 1981. "Post-Disaster Morbidity of the Bereaved: A Possible Role for Preventive Psychiatry." *Journal of Nervous and Mental Disease* 169: 203-212.

U.S. Bureau of the Census. 1985. *Statistical Abstract of the U.S.: 1986* (106th ed.). Washington, DC, p. 73.

2

Grief and Its Effects: Parental Reactions to the Death of an Adult Child

Constance Weiskopf and Mahlon S. Hale

All aspects of grief and bereavement are troubling events in which the loss of a loved one must be assimilated into the lives and altered expectations of surviving spouses, family members, and friends. Whether grief is anticipated and experienced in some sequence that appears appropriate to observers or caregivers or emerges only after some extended period, it is surrounded by uncertain and unpredictable aftereffects. Many referral centers, true to their name, are removed both in space and time from the homes of those who grieve. Physicians and nurses who work in such hospitals, and even those who are in general community oriented hospitals, are inured to the eruption of the emotion that frequently accompanies a patient's death. These workers frequently have little opportunity to observe and understand the grief work itself, a process that extends beyond the patient to other individuals and continues after the patient's death. The experiential process of watching and working with grieving individuals is left to caregivers at home or to researchers who invest time and energy in epidemiologic efforts to uncover the protean manifestations of grief and its differential impact among different classes of survivors. Sometimes, perhaps inevitably, this latter work suffers from what we call the disease of numbers, which causes the individuality of experience to be lost in a larger cohort. Although establishment of this larger group is a prerequisite to the formulation of a baseline of behavior and any expectations about grief and bereavement, all of us know that a sense of what the experience must be like for individuals is lost in the larger scene. We will try to address this problem, presenting the work of our consultation–liaison team with a middle-aged couple both before and after the death of their young adult daughter from a malignancy that began when she was in early adolescence.

Like other caregivers who work with the dying and their families, we also suffer from the disease of numbers. Individual patients in the so-called here and now situation of acute care medicine may be as familiar to the psychiatric consultation service as members of our own families. In fact, the intensity with which we and other physicians and nurses interact with dying patients sometimes exceeds personal experience; it is hard to translate back into a domestic or personal setting just what it is that we are working on or have experienced in the time spent with them or their families. We may also be reluctant to divulge what goes on, not because it is private or arcane, but because we have expended so much energy in the task that recitation seems exhausting and nonproductive.

It is typical to say, if not to believe, that the reaction of spouses to the death of their partners is the predominant focus of attention for aftereffects, but this simply reflects the constraints of adult workers with adult patients. Elsewhere, specifically in pediatric units, the emphasis would be on parental and family reactions. It has not been common for us to observe or work with the parental reaction to a child's death, or at least a family's reaction to the death of a loved one who is still considered a child. When, after all, are we children and when are we adults? Boundaries depend on the perceptions of those who grieve, and such perceptions become even more idiosyncratic when directed to issues of death.

The point of entry for this case involved the psychiatric service's work with a 21-year-old woman who had been admitted many times for the unsuccessful treatment of a sarcoma. We were intensively involved with this patient throughout the last year and one-half of her illness. Two months after our initial contact with her, we arranged a parent meeting. This is an offer we make to all such patients and their families in conjunction with social service efforts, but the offer is not always accepted. These middle-aged parents of five children had been aware of our involvement with their daughter, but had not responded to our invitations until this time. Perhaps this can be attributed to the fact that the patient and her parents had been dealing with the progression of the illness since her early adolescence and had worked with a variety of physicians and supporting caregivers at other hospitals. Thus, it was not so much that our offers had been ignored as that the family had been enmeshed for some time.

In this first meeting, the parents identified the open and supportive character of their relationship with their daughter, their middle child, as a sustaining theme throughout her prolonged illness. We discovered that this had begun to change with their daughter's most recent hospital admission. They felt, for the first time, that their daughter had "cut us off," and that she had begun to exert a curious form of independence not just with respect to her illness but also to her social and college life. This parental assessment was not a heightened emotional response to the increasing severity of the patient's illness; we too had observed a tendency for the patient to cut us off. We interpreted this as a movement toward autonomy, even though it emerged at a time when uncertainty about the course of her illness was most pronounced and her future most unsure.

In addition to feeling separated from their daughter, each parent acknowledged some increased distancing between themselves, so that they were less likely to share their needs and concerns and less able to make joint decisions without acrimony. Of the two, Mrs. Z had become more involved with her daughter, while Mr. Z, after many years, had immersed himself again in several complex hobbies. We speculated that the enveloping character of their daughter's illness had dominated parental consciousness and had become not just the focal point but the long-term topic that bound them together. Apparently, we met the Z's at a time when the illness had finally taken some toll on both. Early in our discussion with them, the Z's were able to identify real anger at their inability to relieve their daughter's pain and suffering over the years. We found this of interest; we had presupposed that their anger and frustration would be focused either on physicians, who had failed to stop the course of illness, or on the disease itself.

We also had an opportunity to work with the patient's maternal grandmother, although this was somewhat limited because of her own poor health. On one occasion, our service team actually visited both the grandmother and the patient on its daily rounds. This older woman, according to her own account, was closer to the patient than to her other grandchildren. She was readily able to verbalize the hopes of the family for this vibrant child on the brink of adulthood, yet painfully aware of the toll the years had taken on her daughter. The grandmother appeared to have a powerful influence on her granddaughter and on her daughter as well, by providing ongoing support while sustaining and reinforcing strong religious beliefs.

Assessment of patient and family thus took into account a broad view of the emotional health of this family and some of the generational support systems that were still in place. One major area of exploration with the Z family was our effort to learn what would be sustaining to them over the long run regardless of the outcome of the illness. In our extended inquiry, we became involved with the family's primary physician who, by this time, was the oncologist, and with his oncology nurse, who had a close—perhaps too close—relationship with the family. We learned that an automatic technique of the Z's had been to incorporate external caregivers into the family, possibly thereby inadvertently signaling the family's lessening ability to adapt to the stresses of the illness. One parenthetical outcome of this incorporation affected the subsequent career change of the oncology nurse, who had regularly visited and dined with the family. Following that patient's death, she resigned her position and went to work with a cosmetic surgeon.

The other sustaining framework for this family was its members' intense religious belief. All were devout Catholics and all regularly sought the counsel of their parish priest. In many respects, this went beyond pastoral counseling. The priest had been in the parish for many years and knew what we learned later—that at one point the mother had had an emotional breakdown. If the pastor functioned as the family's conscience, he certainly was a powerful auxiliary, for their role in relationship to God's plan for them was a powerful, sustaining theme in their grief.

After this initial assessment, substantial time elapsed before the patient's death and our subsequent work with her family. The patient did not die precipitously; the course of the illness dragged on for slightly less than two years. During much of this time, the patient was not critically ill, although she had multiple short admissions. We did follow the parents, as well as the patient, over this course. We learned that the parents' observation about their child's autonomy was correct. The mother clearly identified herself as needing continued, ongoing support, viewing herself as the "conscience" of the family and hence, its chief caregiver. In addition, we learned that years earler, Mrs. Z had had "a breakdown." She viewed her connection with us not just as a means of dealing with the chronic crisis with her daughter, but as a prophylaxis against a repetition of her own illness. As caregivers and psychological specialists, we then recognized that we had, beyond our agenda with the patient, three very manifest agendas with the parents: first, to aid their own reorganization as their now adult daughter tried to take what little control was available over the process of her illness, and second, to help the mother maintain her own sense of balance and capability through the latter part of the illness. Though the mother's anxiety about another breakdown was of less concern to us after her daughter's death, we paid very serious attention to her worries about her mental health because we were uncertain where the boundaries were between reality and her fantasy that she might have another breakdown. The third item on our agenda was to assist the parents to grieve together over the impending loss of their young-adult child from "what might have been to what currently is."

Let us consolidate what our service did in the fifteen months prior to our patient's death that we believe allowed her parents to engage in the work of active grieving and that eventually led them to adaptive coping. Because the patient never moved out of the sick role, there was a delicate balance for her and for her parents between the wished-for autonomy and the fear of regression. The key was to recognize that although the patient was not going to recover, she would continue to fluctuate between these attitudes. For young adults, awareness of their own death causes much frustration and disappointment. Indeed, the sense of unfairness and of being cheated of life

may be greater than at any other developmental stage. We
saw our role as constraining the parents, basically by allowing
them to step back without guilt when the patient seemed to
signal that she wanted this, but encouraging them to move in
when the patient regressed, again without the feeling that
they were inappropriately overwhelming her.

The daughter's need to maintain the balance between
dependence and independence set the stage for us to support
and assist the parents in decision making about the patient,
their other children, and each other. Whether the patient
was in or out of the hospital, she continued in a therapeutic
relationship with our staff with a minimum of weekly meetings.
At the same time, individual meetings were held with the
patient's mother. We believe that sufficient time was given to
address particular issues of grieving. The parents focused
on the impending loss of their energetic child, who had fought
so long to hold on to her existence. They also discovered appropriate ways to maintain their control without undercutting
their daughter's attempt to maintain her own sense of equi-
librium. Pertinent issues included permitting their daughter
to make decisions about continued treatment, witnessing the
loss of her first love, and supporting her decision to stop
her college education. The core issue for this entire family
was, of course, control, albeit control over a decreased number of variables. Although there are individual situations in
which control is exercised exclusively either by the patient
or a physician, in this instance the parents participated as
well, as did their adult child.

The pastoral counselor, primary nurse, oncologist, and
psychiatric team all dealt with their own issues of control by
sharing and openly acknowledging their contributions to the
family at various stages of the illness. This provided the parents with an environment that was reliable and sustaining,
thus avoiding any need for them to deal with issues of control
among the caregivers themselves. We believe this approach led
to their feeling somewhat "welcome" during the terminal stages
of their daughter's illness.

As time progressed, it was openly admitted that the patient
would remain ill until her death. This allowed us to assist the
parents preemptively in dealing with the patient's anticipation
of final regression. For example, the couple discussed openly
and individually with the consultation staff the changing roles
they had been given. The mother discussed her guilt over
having been chosen as confidante by her daughter. The father,
contrarily, found himself having increasing arguments with his
daughter as her death approached. Just before the patient's
death, each parent engaged in dialogue with her alone, and
this, they believed, helped to resolve some of these conflictive
roles they had experienced in the last weeks of her life. It
also allowed them to share their individual roles with their
daughter. As they watched their daughter's body giving up

control, the parents felt less pressured to maintain their own control. Their support systems were in place, and they found family meetings satisfactory forums for all members to share their changing needs and reactions to the impending death.

The patient died on Thanksgiving Day. The day after her death, the mother approached us. She reported that as they left the hospital on Thanksgiving, they looked up into the sky and saw a cloud that looked like a cross. Regardless of any interpretation we might make of this experience, the parents took it as a sign that they could let their daughter go: "She was in God's hands." Immediately thereafter, Mrs. Z requested to continue her meetings with one of our staff on a weekly basis. This therapeutic relationship continued regularly for the next seven months and then intermittently until the first anniversary of her daughter's death. Adjustment to the loss and reestablishment of the marital relationship were key issues. During the second year, she had less regular contacts with us, but these intensified again around the anniversary. We had the feeling, even with the intervals between these latter appointments, that Mrs. Z felt compelled to check with us, possibly for the reasons alluded to earlier.

Other members of the family also continued their relationship with our service, but on a less regular basis. Mr. Z periodically accompanied his wife to meetings with us. He was less verbal than she, and toward the anniversary became moderately depressed and agitated. However, he would never place his interests paramount in the meetings, in spite of encouragement to do so, and we concluded that his primary agenda was not so much his own restitution as it was the continued stability of the relationship with his wife.

The Z's sought out, through their own resources, other families that had lost children. In her discussions with these parents, Mrs. Z felt that she was often alone in her feeling that she and her entire family had "been adequately supported to cope with such a drastic loss." She attributed the difference to the system of care that had been provided. "We experienced," she said, " a system that cared, offered us trust, and never abandoned us. Because of this we felt we had all we needed to sustain us and allow us to go on."

3

Reflections on the Impact of Loss of an Adult Child in the Grief Experiences of Bereaved Parents

Ruth P. Williams

An understanding of the grief experienced by parents of adult children usually encompasses an understanding of aged parents. Parents need their children. Because elderly parents experience physical illnesses and handicaps, including impaired vision and hearing, as well as numerous social problems, parents and adult children often reverse their roles, the children assuming an authoritative position with their parents and the parents becoming dependent on the children. The parents' impairments and the dependence they evoke require understanding and patience from the adult child, who is expected to give strength and comfort (Grollman and Grollman 1978).

When the adult child dies, the parent feels a great void, even if other children survive. The parent feels robbed of a precious jewel, insecure and anxious about the future. Forgetfulness may increase, not necessarily caused by senility, but because the parent is overwhelmed with unexpected problems. Grief exaggerates all other problems. Physical symptoms become more pronounced and medical problems more complicated. Interest may diminish—not only interest in people and things, but interest in eating, caring for oneself, and just living. Mental symptoms may be misunderstood.

The parent whose adult child has died has suffered other losses. Through the years, other loved ones have died, and family and friends have been lost through separation, divorce, and retirement. The aged parent also has experienced the loss of employment, the loss of youth, and the loss of personal possessions, among others.

Therefore, it is imperative that caregivers understand as fully as possible the parent's life situation and the particular place the deceased child held. Being supportive, kind, understanding, and patient—in Grollman and Grollman's (1978:145) words, "listening, sharing, touching, laughing, celebrating [which] can create a loving atmosphere"—is essential in the therapeutic process. Establishing trust in the relationship creates an environment for helping bereaved parents cope with grief. Sometimes professional intervention is required to help bereaved parents handle depression, especially if a parent has suicidal inclinations. The parents' preoccupation with death and dying may indicate their concern with the possibility of their own demise. They need someone to talk to—someone to listen and care—as well as guidance and direction in solving some of the problems presented by the loss.

Four of the five examples of aged parents' reactions to the deaths of their adult children presented in this chapter were actual cases that I, as a funeral director, first dealt with while preparing for their children's deaths or funerals: the fifth case involved a woman who was referred to me by our church. Before the funeral, I encouraged the bereaved families to prepare obituaries that were used in the printed programs of the funeral services. This activity helped them reflect on the children's life histories, achievements, and personal characteristics. The positive images and fond memories that were evoked assuaged their feelings of sadness.

The case materials document the feelings of grief that the aged parents expressed during my in-depth telephone conversations with them after their children's funerals. During these conversations, I encouraged the parents to call whenever they wanted to talk with me and invited them to see me for personal interviews, which many did over the course of the next three years. The cases illustrate many similarities in the parents' experiences and their feeling that this loss was different from all of their other experiences with death, including that of their spouse.

THE P FAMILY

Mrs. P, aged 52, had died from cardiopulmonary failure precipitated by carcinoma of the lung and vulva. Her family failed to follow through in allowing me to discuss their grief reactions with them after the funeral. For three months before Mrs. P's death, her daughter had kept in close contact with me, only by telephone, reviewing her mother's expressed wishes for immediate cremation and expressing her own feelings. I offered to talk with her in person, but she refused. When her mother died, she called me and reiterated her desire to fulfill her mother's request. She and her father had decided to have a brief memorial service following her mother's cremation. Although she agreed to arrange for me to interview her maternal grandparents when they arrived in the city for the memorial service, the meeting never occurred.

Despite innumerable telephone calls to the relatives, especially to Mrs. P's daughter, I was unable to get the desired interview or to communicate with Mrs. P's parents. Mrs. P's daughter had prepared everyone for her death, so they would be able to handle the affairs as she had planned them. Thus, the family "had nothing to do but follow what she wanted, and all is well."

MRS. X

Mrs. X described the sudden death of her only child, a married son who was 60 years old, as a "devastating shock," although she had a premonition of his death. During one of Mrs. X's acute illnesses and hospitalizations, she saw her son daily, as was their custom. Observing his physical symptoms and appearance, she became apprehensive about his well-being and urged him to seek medical attention.

The next day, her son felt unable to come to the hospital to provide transportation for her discharge home. Instead, they visited by telephone and he asked her to postpone her discharge until the following day; she agreed, again expressing concern for his health. Later that day, she telephoned to inquire about how he was feeling and was assured by her daughter-in-law that all was well. That same evening, her son decided he would go to the hospital after all to bring his mother home. At his request, his wife drove him. When they arrived at the hospital, he became acutely ill and was rushed to the emergency room, where he died from pneumonia. Mrs. X was informed of his death the following morning by her physician, who was deeply concerned about her because of her serious heart condition. She said she knew that it was her son when the physician said he had some bad news for her. She had not slept the entire night and had experienced strange feelings.

Three years after her son's death, Mrs. X felt her grief as acutely as when it first occurred. She described feeling alienated, isolated, and depressed, and often felt no desire to live, although she did not think of terminating her own life. Her only solace was the comfort she experienced when reading the Bible or other inspirational literature and when she made her frequent visits to the mausoleum where her son is entombed. These experiences were like oases in a vast desert of despair. Each year, Mrs. X's grief seemed worse. Since her son's death, she had suffered two more heart attacks, the last of which was nearly fatal, and had undergone eye surgery. I initiated contact with Mrs. X through our church because a mutual friend knew of my interest in the bereaved and thought I might be able to offer some help. (I had not been the funeral director of her son's services, which is why I had not had previous contact with her.) When I first began counseling Mrs. X, she was listless and expressed no desire to live.

When speaking of the time since her son's death, Mrs. X said: "Don't tell me that time heals all wounds. I have heard that so much, and it is not true. It takes more than time to heal the hurts if there was real love." She revealed she had no one to listen to her; her friends would change the subject when she tried to express her feelings, urging her to talk about pleasant subjects.

She and her daughter-in-law occupied separate apartments in a two-family house they owned jointly. However, her relationship with her daughter-in-law was strained; they never had good rapport and her grandson had apparently been influenced by his mother's feelings. She had no other relatives except a cousin who did not live in the same city.

Mrs. X had been seriously ill when her son was born. Because she and her husband were not close, she had assumed total responsibility for the child's upbringing, taking him everywhere she went. When she and her husband separated, when the boy was a teenager, Mrs. X and her son became even closer. They were so devoted to each other that they could understand each other's feelings without talking.

After her son's death, Mrs. X could not get him out of her mind. She cried frequently. Deep feelings of loneliness and alienation overwhelmed her, and her depression grew deeper. At times, she was so nervous that she staggered and became forgetful, which made her afraid, for, as she said, "I don't want to lose my mind." Assuring her that others have expressed similar feelings and thoughts, I suggested that we keep in close touch. I further suggested that she come to a group meeting of other women who were experiencing unresolved grief, which she did. Mrs. X expressed positive feelings about the group experience, saying she had been greatly helped. During the group meeting, it was particularly interesting to observe the interaction between Mrs. X and a young widow because it cast some light on Mrs. X's relationship with her daughter-in-law and may have helped her to understand her daughter-in-law's feelings. The group concluded that the loss of a spouse is not the same as the loss of a child, but that each individual's grief response is nevertheless affected by the total relationship.

Often, Mrs. X kissed her son's photograph and said, "I love you" as they used to do in life. She had been using the photograph to communicate with him mentally and found it comforting. I also suggested that Mrs. X talk aloud to her son's photograph. She tried to put questions to him as though he were giving her advice. She did not experiment with speaking out his responses, but she thought about how he would have answered her or what he would have wanted her to do. Also, when she mentally heard him say, "Mom, don't let it get you down," she felt uplifted. Mrs. X remembered that once when she was very ill and it was feared that she would die, her son had said to her, "Don't do this to me, Buddy" (his nickname for her). I suggested that when she felt despondent, she should talk this over with him and recall his words to her. She found this device to be helpful as well.

Sometimes Mrs. X felt that she was not appreciated for anything she had done. Then she became angry at her daughter-in-law and grandchild, both of whom had been recipients of her generosity through the years, but did not appreciate her and thought they were entitled to all she had done and more. Once, while talking about her daughter-in-law, Mrs. X voiced her lifetime desire to have a daughter, which she had originally thought would be satisfied by her relationship with her daughter-in-law. She knew that her daughter-in-law resented her closeness with her son, even though she had tried to allow the couple privacy by remaining in her own apartment except for fleeting visits. Without her son, she sensed even more the need for a daughter, especially for someone to talk with. I suggested that she talk with me as she would with a daughter, and she responded positively. She enjoyed talking to me on the telephone but was afraid of intruding, so I had to initiate calls to make her feel comfortable.

I asked her about her feelings toward God, since I knew she was a devout Christian and a weekly communicant. She said she never felt anger toward God and she knew God makes no mistakes. I told her that after the death of a loved one, it is not unusual for people to be angry at God—that it is an understandable and acceptable human response. Assuring her of God's love, compassion, and forgiveness, I said that God has the compassion to accept us fully as we are. She responded by saying that she read the Bible for inspiration and comfort, particularly the Psalms and the Book of Job. These books gave her so much hope and consolation that she felt able to conquer her feelings of despair. Therefore, when she thought she had conquered these feelings, she was surprised at her sense of futility when she asked, "Why my son instead of me? My days are more over than were his." I responded that there is no answer to "why?" and suggested that posing that question repeatedly might further her frustration and despair. Instead, she should concentrate on the memories she cherished. This became our focus, and, as shown by her improved outlook, the results were encouraging.

She said that she received "a lot of help, comfort, and relief from having someone to listen to her without feeling that she was being a nuisance." She regarded her conversations with me as "enlightening," and said that she had not felt dizzy since our talks began. At the beauty shop, she felt cheerful, too, mainly because her hairdresser was so cheerful. The manicurist who did her nails worked at a different shop, but Mrs. X liked to make this double trip because the manicurist was especially talkative and cheerful, which made Mrs. X feel good. She said that no one wants to be depressed, and she was trying to overcome these feelings; she was especially concerned with being a nuisance. I urged her to reach out more, even if she felt she was being a nuisance, which I assured her she was not, and make calls to me. She always sounded eager to talk, but she was hesitant to initiate contact.

We talked about other daily activities. She ate her meals alone, but she had been accustomed to doing so for many years, and she enjoyed food and cooking. With pride, she reported that she always prepared balanced meals. Although the depression persisted to the point of her feeling "very low in spirits," she was beginning to have more frequent moments of cheerfulness. She even was able to say aloud, as she passed the cemetery where her son was buried, "Hi, sweety," and she felt good.

Impressions

Mrs. X was responding positively to our weekly meetings with each other and our telephone conversations. The group session was helpful, and she was looking forward to being with the group again. Although her sense of futility and depression was not gone, Mrs. X had more frequent moments of relief and joy, which she attributed to the "kindness, patience, and understanding" I offered in our conversations. She felt less alone and relieved just to be able to tell someone about her feelings.

I do not think that Mrs. X needed intensive psychiatric intervention. Even though her expressions of grief were intense despite the three years since her son's death, she had remained at the stage she was in following the funeral because she had not received any intervention. The pastoral calls she received were directed toward her health and the distribution of the sacraments; no attention was given to her desperate cry for help with her grief. During the group session, she met others from diverse backgrounds and age groups who were in various stages of grief. I thought that the young widow in the group would be particularly helpful to Mrs. X in coping with the death of her son and the resulting feelings of loss and grief.

MRS. Q

I conducted interviews with Mrs. Q, whose daughter had died at age 36 as a result of cardiovascular collapse and pulmonary emboli following a lengthy bout of Hodgkin's disease. The daughter had suffered from lupus erythematosis and had been in poor health since the age of 13. After her daughter's death, Mrs. Q's expression of grief included much hostility, and her speech was abrasive, although she talked freely about her feelings. Mrs. Q was so filled with anger that at times she seemed to choke while talking, but she admitted that she had not yet cried and, indeed, had not cried since childhood. Her father used to cry easily, but when he disciplined her, he would "whip her," and she would refuse to cry. However, when Mrs. Q was handling some of her daughter's personal belongings, she finally cried freely. Many times, she felt a lump in her throat and constriction in her chest, especially when she saw young women who reminded her of her daughter. Her anger was directed primarily at the hospital and the physician who attended her daughter, because her daughter had died alone—something that would not have happened if the hospital personnel had called her as she had requested.

Mrs. Q's anger was also directed at God, of whom she could not resist asking "Why?" Her daughter had responded the same way, never being able to accept the limitations imposed by her illness. She always asked, "Why me? Why should I be different from other people?" Mrs. Q's anger caused her to reject the Bible, even though she continued to believe in God and sometimes attended church services. Mrs. Q was bitter that her daughter's former co-workers and friends did not send cards to her daughter while she was ill. Some co-workers and friends visited Mrs. Q a few days after the funeral, but she really did not want to see them and did not appreciate their calls; however, she said that she had been polite and cordial.

Holidays were especially difficult for Mrs. Q. Unable to feel like celebrating, she refused to join the rest of her family in participating in any of the activities that she had previously shared with her daughter. Her entire social and home life were organized around this daughter, who was the eldest of her three children. She and her daughter had lived in the same house, with separate quarters for privacy. They had spent all their free time together and shared many interests. Their relationship was so close that after her daughter's death Mrs. Q felt alone, even though her other daughter and grandchild moved in to be with her. The surviving daughter felt that her mother openly resented the fact that she and the child were occupying the dead daughter's living quarters.

In describing her grief, Mrs. Q said that her daughter's death was the worst loss she had ever suffered. Her parents' and her husband's deaths did not affect her as her daughter's did—this loss was more devastating, but she could not explain how or why.

Four months after her daughter's death, Mrs. Q was still so consumed with hostility and doubts that she was unable to talk about anything else. Her entire attention was directed toward obtaining the hospital records through a court order so that she could learn the truth about her daughter's diagnosis and cause of death. Unable to look at her daughter's photograph because it made her sad, she admitted that she might "break down and cry." When I asked what would happen if she cried, she responded with great determination only that she did not want to do so. Yet, Mrs. Q seemed to find some relief in venting her feelings and talking about her daughter. Most people, including her other two children, did not want to talk about the dead daughter, whose name they never mentioned.

When she was alone, Mrs. Q often "talked to" the deceased, saying such things as, "Wish you were here! I miss you." Work seemed to relieve some of the tensions she felt, and sometimes, on the way home from work, when she had something to share with her daughter as she used to, she would catch herself saying, "Wait 'til I get home to tell you!" Frequently, Mrs. Q felt a "presence" in the house and heard noises when no one was there. She did not "exactly believe in spirits," but she knew she felt her daughter's presence just as she had the night her daughter died. She missed her daughter "more than ever" and felt that "now it is just me." When I reminded Mrs. Q of her other two children, who seemed solicitous and supportive, she responded that her deceased daughter was different, was kind.

Although she acknowledged that she had done all she could for her daughter, Mrs. Q. still wondered if perhaps she could have done more. Anger and hostility were still in the forefront despite our talks, but she seemed less abrasive and more subdued since we had started talking. Her goal remained to seek legal help to obtain the medical records that would document her daughter's illness. Even though her daughter had suffered a lengthy illness, Mrs. Q referred to the death as sudden and unexpected. As in the past, she had thought that her daughter would be discharged from the hospital and return home, and that they would resume their usual activities.

Impression

I believed that Mrs. Q would persist in trying to obtain her deceased daughter's hospital records. Once she gained them, perhaps she would be able to redirect her energies so that she could cope with her grief in other ways. Her focus on the records had helped her to vent her anger, but when her hostility was sufficiently dissipated and she no longer needed to seek vengeance, Mrs. Q might be able to deal more directly with her other feelings and perhaps no longer would refuse to cry. Mrs. Q had been hurt, and she seemed to want to hurt in return. Remaining available to her in a supportive role, I believed, was the best way I could help.

MRS. Y

Mrs. Y's 25-year-old son had been her middle child. Her two older daughters and two younger sons were grown and continued to live with her. She and her husband were separated. Her dead son had seemed healthy, full of energy and vigor, and was involved in many activities. His sudden death from what was thought to be indigestion but was really acute coronary insufficiency upset her beyond description. Nothing had ever hurt her as much as this loss.

When her parents and sister had died, their deaths were expected, and she had been able to accept these losses. When, just two weeks after her sister's funeral, her brother died suddenly from an illness that had not been considered fatal, it was a shock, and her grief had been intense. Her brother had accepted her invitation to live with her after their sister's funeral, but he did not have a chance to do so. Mrs. Y continued to feel that he had been trying desperately to tell her something that she would never know. This had been hard to accept, but her son's sudden death was even more difficult. Not only was his death a shock, but, again, her son had not told her he was not feeling well, and she felt that she "should have known."

Mrs. Y was a religious woman who attended church regularly, read the Bible, and accepted "the word of God." Her faith was what gave her strength and "held her together." She said, "God has helped me through this to give me the light. I don't blame God. At first I questioned why, then I asked for forgiveness for questioning. Some good came because my spirits were lifted, and this made me get closer to God." The church to which Mrs. Y belonged had what they called "nurses' aides" who assisted the pastor in "nursing" parishioners in their grief and other problems. These nurses' aides came often to talk with her, encouraging her to "let it all out" and "trust in the Lord." Her pastor visited often to pray with her. In addition to these supports, Mrs. Y received much love from her children. However, they did not want to talk about their dead brother. Instead, her elder son said, "Mom, let it go." Although the children did not want to hear her speak of his death and told her to get hold of herself, they, too, remembered and, on occasion, would reminisce.

During the earliest period of Mrs. Y's bereavement, she was frequently depressed but was unable to explain how she really felt. She had suffered from hypertension and arthritis for many years, and had experienced pains in her chest and shoulders even before her son's death. Now the pains were more frequent and more severe, but her physicians had not found a cause and referred to her problems as "nerves." In addition, she had frequent bouts of insomnia. Her physical symptoms seemed to be exacerbated when she was most distressed over her son's death.

In the mornings, she would look out the window at her dead son's car, which remained parked in front of the house, and she cried "a lot more." Again, in the evenings, at the time he usually returned home from work, she would expect him and would cry. Pressure in her chest "seemed to come from the bottom of her stomach to her chest." Then she realized that "he is not here any more." During the first two months after her son's death, Mrs. Y could not talk about her son or even hear his name without crying and "choking in her chest." It all seemed like a bad dream, a nightmare. She imagined that it was not true, that it had not really happened. As if in a daydream, she would catch herself waiting for a call from the hospital. To "pull herself together," she tried blocking thoughts and memories of him out of her mind, but found that by doing so she had also blocked out everything else. She was becoming forgetful and repeating herself. Fearing insanity, she fought against these daydreams and began to remember more clearly.

I told her that grieving persons often fear that they are going insane, so that her fears were not unusual. However, she was able to find ways of coping by redirecting her thoughts, which showed strength. Perhaps having more frequent talks with someone she trusted and who would listen to her concerns might be helpful. She thought that the nurse's aides were the most helpful in this regard, and I urged her to continue to use them; I would remain available to her and would contact her intermittently.

Focusing on her feelings of responsibility for her son's death, I elicited more details about her understanding of what had actually happened. She had learned from the coroner's physician that her son had a "twisted artery from birth." Initially, she wondered whether the physicians had the right equipment to treat her son or whether they did their best in the emergency room, but the coroner assured her that nothing more could have been done. Because of the autopsy, she felt better able to accept the cause of his death, which, the coroner's physician explained, was caused by "acute coronary insufficiency due to anomalous origin, right coronary artery." Yet, the questions persisted: "Why didn't he let me know that he was sick? Why wasn't this condition discovered before, especially if he had it from birth? Why was he never sick before?"

Friends told her that her son confided that he was having chest pains and that his feet were swelling, but that he had not wanted to worry his mother. Two days before his death, he told one of his sisters that he might have "flu or indigestion" but that he did not want to worry his mother. He also confided in his girlfriend about his health concerns. These revelations hurt her—that he had confided in others but had not let her know, even though they were close. I suggested, and she agreed, that she felt left out. She wondered whether getting him to a physician earlier would have saved his life— if only she had known. When she was feeling in "good spirits," she realized that her son was protecting her.

The Christmas holidays were the most difficult period for Mrs. Y, coming just one month after her son's death. It did not seem right not to have him with the family; he was always cheerful and everyone liked him. His friends telephoned her and expressed how much they, too, missed him. His supervisor from the large department store where her son had worked also called, saying he still could not believe that her son was gone and that he felt the hurt almost as much as she did. The shipping clerks over whom her son had been foreman called to express their sentiments and to reminisce, as did relatives. She appreciated these calls and concerns and was able to talk freely even though with sadness. However, she was unable to eat during the Christmas dinner: "It just wasn't right for him not to be there."

Four months later, Mrs. Y found that her feelings of deep sadness were less frequent than before. She talked about her son a great deal and thought of him regularly, but with less pain. Her contacts with the nurse's aides from the church continued to be helpful. Moreover, her other children were better able to reminisce with her, even though they still tried to change the subject and to direct her thoughts to other things. Mrs. Y tried to make a "self-adjustment" and to "deal with herself." She was doing much better than she had expected.

Mrs. Y's visit to my office at the funeral parlor to pick up the copies of the death certificate she had ordered was traumatic for her. Suddenly, she felt just as she had on the day she came to make arrangements for her son's funeral. Her chest pains and headache were pronounced, just as they had been then. Although she did not believe that her general health problems were caused by her grief, she acknowledged that the symptoms had worsened since then. Her physicians suggested that the knots she felt in her chest, arms, and shoulders when talking about her son were caused by tension, and that she should think about her own health instead of her son's death. She decided to concentrate on her medical care, but she still knew that she needed to talk about her son as well. She continued to worry about her failure to recognize that he was ill. No measure of explanation by the physicians, family, or friends seemed to allay her feelings. Her only solace came from the nurse's aides of her church, who continued to offer prayer and encourage her to accept what had happened as part of the divine plan.

Impression

Although Mrs. Y's concerns about her failure to recognize her son's illness remained, she seemed to have made progress in handling the deep sadness she felt. She was much less lethargic in speech and more alert and active. However, she seemed to have gone as far as she was able in her contacts with me, and she did not appear to need my services any longer. Her medical needs were more pressing, and she wanted to concentrate on them.

Mrs. Y's health problems seemed to be directly related to her grief. This relationship between grief and ill health parallels the findings of Lynch (1977), who reported studies demonstrating that depression and disease are sometimes linked to the loss of a loved one.

MR. AND MRS. Z

Mr. and Mrs. Z's 33-year-old married son died suddenly several hours after an accidental fall in which he incurred multiple internal and external injuries and lost consciousness. He remained in a comatose state until his death. Many close relatives witnessed the accident and remained close by until the end. Mr. and Mrs. Z, who lived out of the city, came for the funeral and departed soon afterwards. My contacts with Mr. and Mrs. Z (who was the young man's stepmother) were limited to long-distance telephone conversations, but I had more intensive and person-to-person sessions with the son's widow. The five other children in the family maintained close relationships with their parents.

The father spoke little because, as he revealed, he tried to avoid talking about or thinking about his son. It all seemed like a bad dream, unreal, but he knew it had happened. At times, it seemed as though his son were alive. For him, the sudden death of his son was "God's will." He said, "Whatever plan God might have, it was for the best. Perhaps this death was a sacrifice to straighten out the lives of the other children." Yet, he believed he could have more readily accepted his son's death if his son had been ill. Even though he tried to avoid thinking of his son's death, thoughts occasionally returned: "I still have memories, many good ones." He found much comfort in hearing his wife read the obituary from his son's funeral program.

In contrast to Mr. Z, who kept his feelings to himself, Mrs. Z was outgoing and responsive, seeming to welcome the opportunity to share her feelings. She described her relationship with the deceased as close. He was like a real son to her: he was the only one of her stepchildren who called her "Mom" and whom she called her son. He was special, so affectionate and thoughtful, and visited his parents regularly. His sudden death created a void, and Mrs. Z thought she was taking it harder than her husband.

Something about the deceased, which Mrs. Z could not explain, had always caused her to be fearful that he would die a sudden death, perhaps in an automobile accident. Therefore, although his death was sudden and traumatic, she was not surprised; she expected it.

Both Mr. and Mrs. Z thought that "time" had helped them adjust and accept the loss of their son. They continued to feel sad occasionally, but were comforted by their faith, accepting what happened as God's will.

Impression

Mr. and Mrs. Z seemed to have resolved their initial intense grief and appeared to be able to move on with their lives by accepting their son's death and relying on their faith. Their relationship was close and protective, and had been so before the death of their son. Both had medical problems and some physical handicaps that caused them to depend on each other even more. Concern for each other's well-being consumed much of their attention, diverting them from their grief.

THE PARENTS' REACTIONS

The parents of the adult children who died suddenly—one in the emergency room of the hospital from which he was about to take his mother home and the other as a result of an accidental fall—described the initial shock as devastating. The suddenness of these deaths seemed to have blocked out awareness of other details of their children's lives, so that the bereaved parents seemed stuck in the stage of trying to accept the reality of what had happened. In the case of the son who died of coronary insufficiency, the mother was unable to reconcile the fact that her son, who had shared many intimacies with her, had withheld information about his physical problems because he did not want to worry her. The two deaths from chronic illness aroused different reactions in the parents. The death of Mrs. P, who had carcinoma of the vulva and the lungs, had been anticipated for several months. Mrs. P had prearranged her funeral; her parents seemed to have accepted their loss. However, Mrs. Q, whose daughter had been in poor health since the age of 13, responded to the death as though it were sudden and unexpected.

Although the causes of death were different in each case, the parents' grief reactions of disbelief and denial of the reality of death were similar. The parents described imagining that the deaths were a bad dream, that their children were not dead but would again be in their company; they said that they wished to have things as they were before. Despite these similarities, the parents' levels of anger were different. Mrs. Q's anger consumed her energies. She was vehement in her expression of hostility toward the hospital and physicians for "not doing all that could be done" to save her daughter, or at least to alleviate her suffering, and for failing to telephone Mrs. Q in time for her to be with her daughter when she died. Mrs. Z was angry at the landlord for the defective porch that resulted in her son's fatal fall, as well as at the hospital for not responding fast enough to save him. Mrs. Y's anger was directed at the hospital and the physicians who misdiagnosed her son, "whose death might have been avoided." The parents' feelings about God and divine providence also varied. Some were angry at God, others questioned God's action, and one had asked God's forgiveness for daring to question the divine plan.

Relatives were described as only superficially supportive. Even those friends and relatives who remained close and loving deterred the bereaved from talking about the death. Thus, the bereaved felt isolated and rejected. Only Mrs. Z had contacts with friends who were supportive and encouraged her to express her feelings.

In describing their grief reactions, the bereaved parents spoke of the depth of their suffering, the intensely felt inner hurt and pain, as well as tightness in the chest and lumps in the throat. They had no desire to celebrate holidays with their families, especially since all but one of the deaths had occurred around Thanksgiving. Their loved ones were absent, and nothing could fill the void—not even the efforts their children made to console them.

Another notable reaction of the bereaved parents was that, regardless of the cause of the child's death, they viewed the death as premature. They repeatedly asked "Why?" and expressed a sense of futility that was difficult to bear. In all cases, the brokenness of the parents was evident, shown particularly in their physical and medical problems. This fact bears out the claim that "relationships that evolve over the years cannot suddenly be disrupted or destroyed without leaving the person physically changed" (Lynch 1977:197). The death of their adult children seems to have created anxiety and insecurity in the parents, who seem to have been deeply dependent on these children. In three instances, the absence of the spouse, as a result of death, divorce, or separation, resulted in substitution of the adult child to fill the void. Therefore, it seems that the greater the parent's dependence on the adult child, the greater the loss suffered in response to the child's death.

CONCLUSION

Confronting the reality and finality of death is a difficult task, made even more arduous by the acute loneliness and feelings of vulnerability that result from the death of a loved one. Emotional support can reduce this vulnerability, relieve the stresses of anxiety, and bolster courage to cope with the inevitable. Supports offered by church workers, family members, and friends, as well as clergy, funeral directors, and other professionals, help to ease bereaved parents' pain and fears. Human contact is a potent healing force (Lynch 1977), and compassionate, attentive listeners confirm that there are indeed those who care and want to share not only the joys of life but also its pain and sorrow. Those who feel deserted by friends and relatives, such as Mrs. Q and Mrs. X, feel lonely and isolated. Those who are without close, meaningful relationships need to be reassured in their self-worth; such assurance may eliminate the dire emotional and psychological consequences of the loved one's death.

The therapeutic benefits of group sessions for the bereaved have been demonstrated. By discussing their mutual problems of grief and their individual ways of coping, group members are helped to function more effectively, reduce anxieties, and learn alternative ways of handling their problems. Such groups also afford new avenues for companionship. For example, when Mrs. X attended a group session, a young widow, in expressing her feelings, helped Mrs. X to gain some measure of insight into her daughter-in-law's feelings. Her insight may not have turned a negative relationship into a positive one, but it may have afforded Mrs. X a measure of relief and provided a step toward improving the relationship.

Jackson (1977) described the different expressions of grief, among which anger, guilt, and depression are the most prevalent. Anger may be directed toward family members, friends, the clergy, physicians and other health care professionals, and funeral directors, among others. Behind this anger is the grief of losing a loved one. Assisting the bereaved to dissipate their anger helps to alleviate some of the pain and opens the channel for understanding the real cause of the anger. Then the bereaved person is able to cope more realistically with the grief.

Guilt feelings also predominate. Usually they are brought on by situations beyond the bereaved person's control and for which he or she is not responsible. Expressing these feelings may help the bereaved person allay some of the guilt. In the process of making funeral arrangements, many individuals experience a release of their guilt feelings because they feel they are doing something for the deceased. The ceremonies and rituals involved in funerals, including viewing the body; visits by friends, relatives, and others; the funeral or memorial service; and the burial or cremation, all provide opportunities for emotional expression by relatives and friends, as well as the bereaved family (Jackson 1977).

Depression can be a serious symptom in grief and may require psychiatric intervention. What can one offer to a bereaved parent who fails to recognize or refuses to accept this kind of professional help? In the management of grief, much can be accomplished simply by being there and accepting the individual as he or she is—with kindness and understanding, compassion and love. Patience, attentive listening, and caring are therapeutic for the grieving person. They are the elixir that bereaved people need to help them over the depths of their grief. Responding to their cries for help and hearing the voices of those who weep are ways of keeping the covenant with those who mourn.

REFERENCES

Grollman, E. A., and S. H. Grollman. 1978. *Caring for Your Aged Parents*. Boston: Beacon Press.

Jackson, E. N. 1977. *The Many Faces of Grief*. Nashville, TN: Abingdon Press.

Lynch, J. J. 1977. *The Broken Heart: Medical Consequences of Loneliness*. New York: Basic Books.

4

The Death of an Adult Child, Acute Grief, and a Closure to Parenting

Richard M. Cohen

In my recent work with the mother of a 28-year-old woman who had tragically died subsequent to medication abuse, I was struck by the therapeutic issues ensuing from the fact that, although her child had been an adult, much of the unfinished business was related to a lack of closure of the parenting process. By this I mean that in the usual course of events, a parallel development takes place for parents and children. For children, there are expectations that with the end of high school and entry into young adulthood, there will be a separation based on a sense of their own identity, competence, and sense of worth that permits them to function independent of parental direction and support. Although the bonds are never completely broken, psychological independence accompanies geographic, fiscal, and social independence. In addition, the attachments are shifted and new connections with other persons are made. Marriage, friendships, and bonds with colleagues may replicate earlier affectional ties. For parents, the parallel development is a sense of some closure to the task of parenting. They achieve some sense of satisfaction, albeit at times ambivalent, that they have provided material support, experiences, as well as a psychological armamentarium that will enable their child to cope with life as he or she moves toward increased independence and self-reliance. For parents, there is also a process of coping with the sense of loss that emerges as their child moves away. They feel not only sadness and joy, but also anger, particularly if the child has not met the standards they would have set for themselves. Thus, my focus is upon a specific form of "unfinished business": the tasks of parenting in the parent-child relationship.

Before I expand this concept, it is important to note that I am not proposing that the issue of parenting is the only issue of relevance for grief at the loss of an adult child. Variables such as the age and gender of the child, the age of the parent at the time of the death, whether the child's death was expected or unexpected, and whether the parent is the mother

31

or the father, all certainly have an impact on, and an inter-
relationship with, the process of grieving. My goal in high-
lighting parenting and related issues is to emphasize the
relevance of the issue to the process of working therapeutically
with bereaved parents.

Four professional colleagues recently experienced the
death of adult children from sudden unexpected causes. Although all of them were distraught and grief stricken by their
loss (and, in some instances, unwilling to discuss details),
each expressed feelings or made statements that indicated that
there is a range to the concept of closure of parenting. Each
indicated that the death revived old issues about whether they
had "done enough" for their child. In particular, they were
concerned about whether earlier parent-child interactions had
in some way been influential in leaving their child vulnerable
to the occurrence of the unexpected death. Thus, guilt and
magical thinking were related to concerns about the suffi-
ciency of parental input.

It is against this background that my work with one client,
whom I shall call Sarah, highlighted the problems that she
was experiencing in resolving her grief, loss, and unwilling-
ness to separate from her dead daughter. At each session with
her, much of the material produced focused on the unfinished
business of the parent-child relationship. This material
reflected the mother's sense of not having successfully achieved
a closure to her parenting of her daughter. Here the issue of
psychological closure is of prime importance. For although her
daughter was relatively self-sustaining in that she had her own
apartment and an acceptable job and had developed a group of
friends who served as a support group, Sarah was essentially
unsatisfied with each of these resolutions her daughter had
achieved and thus, in the sense in which I am discussing it,
believed that her job as parent had not been completed.

In this sense, if incomplete parenting exists within the
bereaved parent, then this becomes a focus in the process of
intervention to facilitate the completion of grief work. Several
examples are illustrative. Sarah perceived her young adult
daughter as being withdrawn, moody, and traveling with a
group of friends of whom she did not approve. Through
continual nagging, she convinced her daughter to seek medical
help. This connection, *as perceived by the mother*, was the
beginning of her daughter's "downfall." The physician pre-
scribed psychotropic medication for the daughter. According
to Sarah, her daughter became addicted to the drug and
eventually died by taking an overdose of it. Sarah's presen-
tation focused on her inadequacy as a mother and her inability
to provide her daughter with the psychological and emotional
support that would have enabled her to cope more successfully
with the stress in her life.

The death of a child, then, is an injury to one's narcissism
and omnipotence as a parent. No matter how realistically one

views the influential nature of parenting, there is a sense of
a direct one-to-one correlation between parental sanction and
child behavior. Thus, at the death of an adult child, the
questions are, "What might I have done differently?" and "Why
did I ever let this happen?" There is a sense of wishing to
change the past, since the present and future will now be
unchangeable.

This issue is related to issues raised by Pincus in her
book *Death and the Family* (New York: Vintage, 1974), which
describes patterns of interaction in marriage. The projective
and identification patterns she describes seem relevant to
parents and children as well. In the death of a child, the
parent sees not only the loss of a biological part of self, but
also the loss of psychological aspects of self that, through
projective identification by the parent or through identification
and introjection by the child, have also died.

In the case of my client, my speculation is that in part,
her distress at her daughter's death was related to her sense
of the death of her own "rebellious self." Although Sarah had
essentially been a conformist, living by the rules, her rebellious self was given life through her projective identification
with her daughter. In addition, it was this part for which the
daughter was punished by death, just as Sarah herself was
punished when she acted in a rebellious way by leaving her
husband and children and eventually obtaining a divorce.
Sarah viewed her daughter's difficulties as her punishment
for having rejected her family when she acted in a way contrary to others' expectations but in a way consonant with her
own needs. Thus, the unresolved aspect of her parenting was
that she had been unable to reconcile the rebellion against
conformity within her daughter and parental expectation of
conformity. A goal of treatment then became to reconcile her
conflict between the part of her that wished to be less rigid
and less bound by external standards and the part that con-
formed; in analytic terms, to reconcile the conflict between
her superego and id or, in transactional terms, her own in-
ternalized parent and child.

A related issue is that of control of the child's behavior
by the parent and the sense of responsibility for this control.
This conflict between control of the child for the gratification
of one's own needs and control of the child for the satisfaction
of the child's needs are highlighted by another example. Upon
returning from a vacation with her husband, Sarah had a
sense that she should stop at her daughter's apartment. Rac-
ing up the stairs, she found her daughter gazing out the
front door in what seemed to her to be a trance. Seeing her
mother, the daughter cried, "Mommy, Mommy." Sarah, seeing
her daughter's trancelike state and disheveled appearance,
begged her daughter to come home with her. The daughter
said she would not come home because once she was there her
mother would not permit her to leave. The mother suggested

a bargain, saying that if the daughter would return with her, she could leave when she wished—the basic conflict again between parental and child control.

In this instance, Sarah acquiesced to her daughter and relinquished her own sense of control. She brought her daughter home and, as she told it, helped her to get cleaned up, took her to the beauty parlor, and then returned to the family home for rest. Sarah then realized she was in a bind. She and her husband had been invited to a Christmas party that was to take place that afternoon. She presented this to her daughter who made no complaint. In fact, Sarah and her husband went to the party for only a few hours and returned home. Not long after their return, the daughter reneged on her part of the bargain and returned to her own apartment.

In a session with me, Sarah berated herself for not having remained with her daughter; she should not have attended the party. She had, in fact, taken control back by deciding to attend the party. The party also fulfilled her own need for some satisfactions. If she had only stayed with her daughter, she cried, she might have helped her, she might have gotten through to her. What is a party anyway? Why did she listen? Why did she have to go? Since there is little reason to believe that these few hours would have had the effect Sarah fantasized, my approach was to play good parent and give her permission to attend the party. I further suggested to her that it would be helpful to her to look at how frequently she cast situations as black or white, all good or all bad, ignoring the greys and human imperfections. I also suggested that perhaps she was also angry at her daughter, and that the respite of the party was a chance for her to regroup her feelings. She said she heard the point, but was not yet ready to forgive herself for her behavior. A really good mother would not have acted that way.

One of my colleagues whose son had died expressed the other side of this coin. In retrospect, she indicated that she realized that she had really had much less control over her son's life than she had felt she had when he was alive. As she expressed it, she realized that she was less omnipotent as a parent than she was ready to accept while she was still actively involved in parenting. Sarah has yet to come to this point. She cannot yet forgive herself for some of her decisions and behaviors, continue to feel guilty for others, and accept the fact that we are all imperfect as parents. She has not yet acknowledged that at some point the control was no longer hers, but rested with her daughter, who, for reasons we will never completely understand, found the control of her own life difficult to achieve.

When less traumatic circumstances surround the final tragedy with a child, and when the child was one who was better able to accept control, the revived incomplete parent-child issues might be less pressing and less central for the parents.

However, my colleagues who suggest that this is so also suggest that for parents to be satisfied that they did all they might have for their children during their formative years is a position most difficult to attain. As one bereaved colleague phrased it, "You are different, and you find it difficult to tolerate who you are at this time. You must grieve for who you *were*, because now you are absolutely different. You feel the pain and learn to live with it."

In summary, there are several levels for the focus of intervention: (1) the attitudinal level in which parents accept that they did the best they could; (2) the psychodynamic level, involving exploration of the unfinished or resurrected aspects of the parenting process; and (3) the emotional level, in which parents find a way to live with the pain, and achieve the reintegration of self, including the projections, identifications, self-ideals, and self-worth that have all been terribly and unequivocally disrupted by the death of an adult child.

5

Parental Loss of
an Adult Child

William V. Hocker

"And thy own soul a sword shall pierce," said the prophet Simeon to Mary, the mother of Jesus, in anticipation of the death of her son (Luke 2:35). These simple and dramatic words could hardly have been more descriptive of the effects of the death of an adult child on parents.

The writer Mark Twain had a daughter named Susy, who died of meningitis at age 24. Ten years later, he said, "It is one of the mysteries of nature that a man all unprepared can receive a thunder stroke like that and live" (Kaplan 1966, p. 335). The anguish experienced by parents has been recorded throughout history.

Since there would be no need to examine the effects of this particular type of death if all deaths were the same, the primary intention of this chapter is to focus on how the death of an adult child differs from other deaths in terms of the intensity of grief experienced by parents. We will discuss the fact that because such deaths are an unnatural interruption of the normal life cycle, a rupture of a unique relationship, they are therefore devastating to the parents. Further, such deaths are frequently sudden and traumatic, and these circumstances greatly compound the normal mourning process and affect the severity and duration of parents' grief. It is necessary for caregiving individuals to understand this type of death in order to be helpful to those who grieve. Since understanding leads to solutions, this chapter will try to contribute to the understanding of the death of an adult child and to make some substantive observations that may be helpful to caregivers in their daily work.

Because there is little information about this *specific* area, the methods used to gather information for this chapter fall into three categories: (1) observations made during years of experience as a funeral director, (2) interviews, and (3) review of what general material does exist on death, dying, and bereavement. All of these methods were helpful, but the interview method was the most revealing, and thus is worthy of

further mention. Approximately one dozen parents were interviewed, too few to achieve any kind of scientific or statistical
validity. However, the purpose of the interviews was merely
to gain insight and to confirm or contradict information gained
from other sources. Nevertheless, there was an extremely high
degree of basic agreement and similarity of response among
those interviewed, as shown by the answers to our questions
and reactions relating to the deaths. The information learned
from the interviews proved to be enlightening and somewhat
unexpected. A list of questions that served as guidelines for
the interviews is included at the conclusion of the chapter.
The questions were not intended to be all-inclusive, but to
provide a framework for conducting the interviews.

For the purposes of this chapter, 18 to 35 will be considered the most common ages for an adult child to die. The
lower age of 18 was chosen because it is the age of majority
in most states; however, the upper age is not necessarily limited to age 35—we did interview one 90-year-old woman who
had lost her 58-year-old son in a firearms accident 12 years
before, when she was 78.

To begin with, the loss of an adult child is an unnatural
break in the normal sequence of events in the cycle of human
life. Nature has its cycles and seasons. Thus, a plant grows,
matures, and produces seeds of its own. The new seeds fall
to the ground full of life as the old plant begins to die. In
the animal kingdom, a newborn deer grows, matures, gradually feels its strength, and fathers or bears strong offspring.
It loses its strength over the years until it succumbs to the
severity of winter or the unrelenting claws of a predator (who
is, in turn, seeking to perpetuate its own kind). And so it
is with humankind. The cycle of nature is geared to the growing strength of the young and the diminishing strength and
eventual disappearance of the old. The whole scheme of nature
is jolted out of its natural cycle by the death of an adult child.

The death of a loved one is one of the primary traumatic
experiences in human existence. The death of an adult child
is a deeper and more pronounced trauma because it involves
the added complication of being contrary to the normal life
cycle. Parents do not usually outlive their children; children
normally live longer than their parents. For these reasons,
the psychological effects of the death of an adult child are
extremely difficult for parents to accept. We are dealing with
the interruption of normal patterns and cycles. This interruption or failure to live a normal life span is often expressed
in sentiments such as: "Why couldn't it have been me instead
of her? I'm old and sick and have already lived my life," or
"He was just getting started." In the Book of Samuel, the
death of King David's son, Absalom, almost destroyed him.
He had been greatly worried about his son because he was
engaged in battle. It is recorded that when he finally learned
of his son's death, "the king was shaken and went up to the

room over the city gate to weep. He said as he wept, 'My son Absalom! My son, my son Absalom! If only I had died instead of you'" (2 Sam. 19:1).

Those who have achieved a certain maturity in age have lived at least most of a normal lifetime. However, young adults who have died were not able to live a normal span. This waste and futility adds to the sense of grief that is felt and expressed by parents. Two of the women interviewed had lost sons to cancer, both of whom were in their thirties and engineers. Other parents interviewed had had children with advanced scholastic degrees who were being very beneficial to society. We were called on to prepare the body of a young man who had been killed in an automobile accident for shipment back home. I spoke to his father on the telephone. The boy had just finished medical school, had been home for a short visit, and was on his way back to school for the graduation ceremonies. The father was justifiably despairing. Once again, we have the theme of waste and a curtailed life span. One person said that the diapers, the braces, the music lessons, the contact lenses, the education had all resulted in waste and futility. Another man said that he and his wife no longer bought things with an eye to leaving them to their child as "family heirlooms." There was no longer anybody to leave them to.

We all feel the uncertainty of life, but none more so than those who have lost an adult child in whom they had invested their hopes and dreams for the future. What more stunning reminder of mortality is there? Those parents who feel that their children are going to take care of them in their declining years lose whatever security they had—if the children die, who is left? What will happen to them? A child's death also contributes to a poor self-image and takes away some of the ego reinforcement that an adult needs to feel secure, worthwhile, viable, and stable. "The proof of our own worth is very important after such a loss" (Schiff 1977: 55).

Another major consideration, in addition to the break in the natural cycle, is that the parent-child relationship is unique: the child is both a flesh-and-bone extension and a psychological extension of the parent. A child is someone a parent raises through hardships and difficulties. Parents love and nurture their child in a way that they do for no other human being. A mother physically carries the child until its birth. A father carries the child psychologically, as shown by the well-documented morning sickness that many fathers experience. Raising a child is part of a parent's entire life's work. The relationship is simply different from any other human relationship and, consequently, the death of a child stuns the parents and results in more intense grief than any other loss.

An almost universal comment from the parents interviewed was that losing a child was like losing a part of oneself. Schiff

(1977) said, "To bury a child is to see part of yourself, your
eye color, your dimple, your sense of humor, being placed in
the ground." This observation that a child is psychologically
an extension of self for a parent has significant ramifications.
For instance, because a child is an extension of self, the death
of a child diminishes that self. As John Donne wrote, "Any
man's death diminishes me, because I am involved in mankind;
and therefore never send to know for whom the bell tolls; it
tolls for thee" (Meditation 17). If the death of other persons
does sadden and diminish a human, then how much more are
parents diminished by the death of their own child? This is
the death of something that a parent has created and is continuing to create. It involves a deep emotional trauma because
of the bonding that exists in a parent-child relationship. A
part of the parents themselves has died; it is as though the
parents are not fully alive any more. In fact, many psycho-
analysts do not distinguish between the personalities of the
child and the mother during the first few months after birth.
So much is the mother's life tied up with the child's that they
consider the personalities to be practically coextensive. Cameron
(1963: 53) has said that a newborn infant is "functionally
parasitic," and that it is only as it grows and interacts with
its mother that it develops "the internal organization of a rudi-
mentary ego system." The "symbiotic mother-child unit" is
such that the child's personality cannot develop properly without interaction with the mother. This is an involved issue that
is only mentioned here in passing to strengthen the point that
a child is an extension of self for a parent—mentally, psychologically, and emotionally, as well as physically.

Many parents live vicariously through their children. This
is evident when a mother pushes her daughter to be an actress
or a ballerina, or when a father expects his son to excel in
athletics. Thus vicarious living is eliminated by the child's
death. Moreover, people desire to leave something of themselves on earth. What better way is there than to leave a child—
one's seed, one's blood? This living legacy represents our
dreams and hopes for the future. Obviously, this instinct is
frustrated when the child dies, and a feeling of hopelessness
may ensue.

The aspect of ego involvement also has other negative
possibilities. Since a child is a source of ego reinforcement,
the death of the child can diminish that ego. There is always
the possibility of self pity because of the way that the loss
will affect the parent, as well as the possibility of embarrassment because of the cause or circumstances of the death.
Human motivations and reactions are very complex, but we
can say that negative and selfish reactions are part of almost
all grieving.

In my observations as a funeral director, I have found
that the emotional reactions to these deaths are much more
intense than those to most other deaths. Fitzgerald (1984: 32),

who has worked in a grief crisis program, said that "the death of a child, whether it be a young child or an adult child, is one of the most severe grief reactions to endure." This observation was borne out by my interviews with parents. Those interviewed felt that the loss of a child caused deeper emotion than other such experiences. One very stoic individual said that he had looked at the deaths of his father and brother with a somewhat unruffled objectivity, but that when his daughter died it was completely different. His feelings then were characterized by intense despair, confusion, and frustration.

Obviously, the death of a loved one is never without trauma if the deceased was truly loved. However, the death of an elderly parent or grandparent is to be expected in the normal course of events. The death of a brother or sister, aunt or uncle may or may not be expected, but the emotional reaction is generally not as severe because the relationship is not as intimate. But what of a mate? The death of a mate seems to be the only death that can rival the death of a child in terms of depth of emotional trauma. This idea was explored in interviews with those who had lost both a mate and an adult child. The results were interesting. When asked directly if the death of an adult child was worse than the loss of a mate in terms of levels of grief, the answers showed amazing agreement. Some said that a husband or wife could be replaced, but a child could not. Others experienced a difficult married life and consequently felt the child's death more deeply. One woman observed that "at least somewhere in the back of your mind you realize that one day you may lose your husband, but you never expect your children to die before you." This observation should not be underestimated because of its simplicity and obviousness: it was an often-repeated theme and carried with it great emotional pain. Another woman said she had not raised her husband but that she had raised her child, a reference, once again, to the unique relationship. It has been felt by many that the death of a mate is the most difficult to overcome. The interviews indicate that this is not necessarily true.

Another point for consideration is that the intensity of this type of loss may bring about changes in the normal grief cycle. The resolution stage is likely to be longer and more severe. When the parents interviewed were asked if they had recovered from the death, the answers were not very positive. At the time of the interviews, the deaths had occurred from three months to twelve years previously. The *most* positive answer to this question was "Yes, but the sense of loss stays with you." Most other comments were not as encouraging. Some said "yes and no." Two others commented that one simply learns to live with the loss, but does not get over it. Finally, one woman said that one does not get over it, just further away from it.

Since the severity and duration of the grief is likely to be more intense, a pathological grief response is also more likely. We will use two possibilities to illustrate this concept. The first is that ego-involvement with the child before death can mask some hidden inadequacy in the parent, so that the child's death can become a catalyst that removes the mask, causing the parent's personality to deteriorate. The second possibility, which is similar to the first, was indicated by Jackson (1957: 20) when he said, "Abnormal grief may involve a situation where the severe loss caused by the death of a loved object may precipitate personality change or adjustment that could bring on a state of depression. This may be true when a person has so overinvested his emotional capital in another that he is destroyed as a person in the loss of this other."

The different emotional feelings we all have are frequently magnified at the time of the death of a loved one. Parents can experience a feeling of guilt, perhaps because they feel indirectly responsible for the death. This can happen, for instance, if parents feel they have unduly influenced their children by insisting that they take a certain type of employment or that they do or do not marry. The circumstances of the death can be related to a decision the parent has made. This can occur, for example, if a child dies in an automobile accident on the way home from college if the parent has pushed the child to go to college. Guilt is often manifested as hostility. Jackson (1957: 20) said, "Hostility may be an effort to protect oneself against his own feelings. Guilt often shows up as anger against others, a substitute for anger against oneself." Funeral directors as well as other caregivers often encounter anger and suspicion with this type of death, particularly on initial contact with the family. On one occasion, a father who had just lost a young girl to leukemia after a long struggle came into our facility and pushed the door open so vigorously that it hit the wall. He had a piece of crumpled paper in his hand, which he threw on the floor. This was totally rude and hostile behavior. We were then and are still good friends. He was merely reflecting the initial anger of the moment. One of those interviewed said she was angry with everybody, including her husband and God. She did not want to talk about her son's death because she felt that those who talked to her were intruding on her grief. She commented later that this reaction was probably selfish: "I guess you could say I was enjoying my grief." Of course, these reactions are also present in response to other deaths, but they are likely to be more intense after the death of an adult child.

Some people never recover from the death of their child. In speaking again about the death of his daughter, from which he and his wife never recovered, Mark Twain said "The cloud is permanent now" (Kaplan 1966; 339). Shakespeare's *King Lear* is considered a tragedy ultimately because of the death of the king's youngest daughter, Cordelia, who hanged herself. In anguish, he cries out

No, no, no life!
Why should a dog, a horse, a rat, have life,
And thou no breath at all?

(Act V, iii)

Lear is old and feeble, and dies soon after Cordelia, not having the strength to overcome this loss. Unfortunately, this is a common occurrence. Also unfortunately, the death of adult children is a common occurrence.

In attempting to understand the grief reaction, it is helpful to understand some of the elements that are operative in the recovery from grief. Although there is no longer a living attachment between the parent and the deceased child, this does not mean that there is no relationship at all. Steele (1983) has said, "At the time of death, the detailed implications of the loss have not yet become real to the survivor. Emotionally the bereaved is still attached to the deceased."

Funeral directors have stood by caskets countless times with survivors who have audibly spoken to the deceased and said, "I love you." They were speaking in the present tense. The emotional or psychological attachment still exists after death and is, perhaps, necessary. To illustrate, Parkes (1972) speaks of "mitigating behavior" that is, essentially, a defense mechanism to enable the bereaved to endure the loss initially. This is accomplished when a bereaved person knowingly permits self-deception. It involves "a sense of the continued presence of the deceased, a clear visual memory of him, and preoccupation with thoughts of him" (Parkes 1972; 59). One woman, speaking of her dead husband said, "He's with me all the time. I hear him and see him although I know it's only imagination. If I didn't take a strong hold on myself, I'd get to talking with him" (Parkes 1972; 59). Intellectually, of course, she realized that her husband was dead, but the emotional attachment still existed and was nurtured by the survivor to enable her to cope.

Steele (1984; 14) has also said, "Intellectually, also the bereaved is unable to fully define the details of the loss. These realizations will only occur with time and intensive confrontation with reality." This could be called psychological "distancing." The more time that comes between the person and the loss, the more recovery is enhanced. This is illustrated by another quotation from Mark Twain: "Susy's death was like a man's house burning down—it would take him years and years to discover all he had lost in the fire" (Kaplan 1966; 337). As time passes, the details of the loss become more clear and, consequently, easier to accept as reality is gradually confronted. We conducted the funeral for a young adult woman whose father was in charge of the arrangements. It

was a long time before we were paid, but when we finally received his check, he enclosed a note, which said that he was
sorry it had taken him so long to pay the bill, but that he
just hadn't been able to write the check and forward it to us
because, to him, it represented the finality that his daughter
was indeed dead. It was not a matter of money; it was simply
a matter of time before he could confront the reality and
finality of the death.

To summarize, the parent-child relationship is ruptured
by death. The relationship or attachment, although finished
physically, still exists emotionally. Time is necessary for the
bereaved to realize emotionally that the deceased is no longer
alive and to realize the details of the loss. The ability to confront reality grows stronger with time in a healthy grief
response, so that mitigating behavior is no longer necessary.

At some point, parents must decide if they *want* to recover
and to resume living in a meaningful way. It is possible that
this choice cannot be confronted for some time, but ultimately
it must be done, often by conscious choice, before resolution
is possible. One woman who was interviewed was shocked into
reality when her dead son's twin brother had to seek therapy
to cope with his brother's death. She decided that it was time
to make the conscious choice to go on with her life. If we define the resolution of grief as a return to normal, healthy relationships and functioning, most parents do recover. "When the
mourning process has been completed, the mourner is usually
a more sober and sometimes a sadder person that before; but
he is ready and able to resume normal interpersonal relationships with other people" (Cameron 1963; 76).

The grief reaction to the loss of an adult child has a
great number of variables because of the diverse circumstances
that exist and that can affect the grief reaction. Some of
these that can be suggested for further investigation are:
(1) age of child, (2) sex of child, (3) sex of parent, (4) marital status of child, (5) marital status of parents, (6) number
of surviving brothers and sisters, (7) degree of family intimacy
(8) religion, (9) ethnic origin, (10) place of death, (11) suddenness of death, and (12) cause of death. The cause of death
is one of the most significant of these.

The two leading causes of death for people between the
ages of 20 and 30 are automobile accidents and suicide. The
parents have to cope not only with the fact of death, but
with a cause of death that is often an embarrassment to them.
"Unless there are extenuating and deep-seated guilt feelings,
it is easier to cope with a child's death from a physical ail-
ment than from an accident" (Schiff 1977; 40). The suddenness
and unanswered questions associated with an accident are very
difficult for parents. They express their added frustration by
asking questions such as "What was she doing there? Why was
she on her way to that place? Why was she with those people
she hardly ever associated with?" The unexpectedness of other

types of accidents, as well as that of death by homicide or drug overdose, is difficult to accept. A father discussing the death of his son 24 hours earlier in a mining accident stated in simple bewilderment, "I don't know which way to turn."

Suicide is the second leading cause of death among college students. Death by self-execution is a great affront to those who remain. In a recent survey sponsored by the National Research and Information Center in Evanston, Illinois, it was found that "100 percent of funeral directors indicated that suicidal deaths produced responses that were in some way different. When asked if they felt the survivors of suicide had experienced shame or embarrassment that was not observed in other types of deaths, 83 percent of the directors said yes. Eighty percent of the responding funeral directors indicated that the funeral itself or events surrounding it were somehow different in the case of suicide" (Calhoun, Selby, and Steelman 1983). This, obviously, is a subject in itself, but can be important in studying the grief reactions of parents.

The title of this chapter implies that there is a possible difference between the death of an adult child and that of an adolescent child. There do not seem to be many basic differences except the obvious ones, which are simply based on the age achieved. Adolescent children are not established in the world as firmly as adult children, and their lives have not achieved either the economic or social complexity of older children's. The adult child, on the other hand, is likely to be entrenched in a career and a family.

If the adult child is married, there is a spouse to consider, a spouse who may not have amicable relations with the parents of the deceased. If there are children, they are a further concern. What will happen to the grandchildren if the surviving spouse remarries? Will the grandparents still be permitted to see them? Do they have to raise them or finance their educations? One man interviewed, whose daughter had died, was very concerned about his future relationships with his grandsons, since his relationship with his son-in-law was not good. There are other issues. Was a deceased daughter pregnant (one of those whose parents we interviewed was)? Was a dead son's wife pregnant? Did a divorced child leave children? Of the many possibilities, these are mentioned simply to point out differences between the death of an adult child and an adolescent child and their potential to exacerbate the grieving process. However, other difficulties are peculiar to the death of an adolescent. The chief of these is probably having to deal with surviving siblings, who often feel the death of a brother or sister very deeply.

In the economic sphere, adolescent children have not had the training and education or the time invested in them that adult children have had. The adult child may have property to dispose of, loans to pay, and a house or car to sell. These complexities can make matters worse. To return to our basic

proposition, the components in the death of a child of any
age are the same. As Schiff (1977: 4) said, "It does not appear to make a difference whether one's child is three, thirteen, or thirty if he dies. The emotion in each of us is the
same."

The people interviewed were asked what helped them to
cope with the death in the short term and in the long term.
We defined short term as the first two weeks after the death
and the long term as anything after that. Their observations
may be able to help us to understand their grieving process.

Regarding the short term, almost all parents said that the
support they received from others immediately after the death
helped. Sometimes these people were friends or relatives who
had travelled long distances to be with them, and sometimes
they were friends from work or church. Many felt encouraged
by the expressions of sympathy, the food brought to the
house, and the flowers sent to the funeral. All were disoriented
and numb following the death but, for most, the viewing of the
body and the funeral service itself were comforting or therapeutic. The realization that the deceased did not have to
suffer any more helped those whose children died of lingering
disease. A personal acquaintance with the funeral director and
confidence in the director's ability to handle arrangements
properly also helped. One man was so frustrated that he began to take long walks with his dog to relieve his despair,
and this helped him. Also, in the short term, he decided just
to try to get by one day at a time.

In the long term, religion helped some people. For example,
one woman said that religion was the only thing that held her
together after her child's death. However, religion did not
seem to help everyone, even some who were active in their
churches or synagogues. The realization that the deceased
would never have to mourn a loved one helped. One couple
said they eventually overcame much of their grief by learning
to enjoy the present and not to look too far into the future.
Some said talking about the deceased and the death to friends
and relatives proved therapeutic both in the short and long
term. And, of course, several said that self-help groups and
talking to parents who had experienced similar loss was helpful.
When asking for suggestions for others who suffered the loss
of a child, the answers were:

Find a good friend to talk to.

Take an interest in something else or someone else's welfare

Stay busy.

Engage in some vigorous physical activity.

Join a self-help group, such as Compassionate Friends.

Don't do anything in a hurry. Don't sell the house or the

car and don't move out of town. It can wait. No matter how together you think you are, you aren't.

Seek counseling if you feel you are not recovering after a reasonable period of time.

Learn to enjoy the present.

Don't deny that you have experienced a major blow, but don't permit it to overcome you.

An unexpected spinoff of the interviews was that they were helpful to parents who had lost a child. Many of the parents simply had not had the opportunity to express their feelings before. Talking about the loss can be a painful and delicate experience, and some of the participants wept. However, they all seemed glad to talk and, even though it was difficult, it was good for them.

A final point confirmed by the interviews is that a great danger in any type of severe grief reaction is to allow oneself to be conquered by the death. An experienced caregiver can recognize this danger, which is best illustrated by a story: "A young woman who suffered from her son's death confessed that when the news came, she quit living. On her son's birthday she resolved to spend the entire day at the cemetery. On her way she stopped at a florist's to buy a wreath. The gray-haired florist was fussing with a dried up plant when she entered. He kept plucking dried leaves from the shriveled stalk. 'Why fuss with that thing,' she snapped. 'It's dead.' The florist glanced up. 'You're wrong,' he said gently. 'Part of this plant has died, true enough. But the rest is healthy tissue. See this green stalk here? The plant will live for many years yet. It will bear pretty flowers too' (Droke 1955:124). Although it may seem to bereaved parents that their lives are dead and meaningless, they must come to the point where they see that there is life left in them and around them that must be lived. As Schiff (1977: xiv) said, "The death of a child is frequently called the ultimate tragedy. But it is a tragedy that must not be compounded by allowing everything around you to die also. There are other children, mates, sisters, brothers, friends, who need and deserve to see you functioning well."

A few years ago, the poet Robert Frost was asked what his response would be if he were asked to sum up all his knowledge in three words. He said, simply, "Life goes on." There never has been, nor will there ever be a pill to obviate grief, to make it go away magically so that the bereaved can avoid the pain of grief. It is a process that must be passed through. Because the cycle of life and death *does go on*, it is necessary that those who suffer this kind of loss go through this immensely difficult, yet *normal* and *necessary* mourning period and be gently pointed to the simple truth that "life goes on." Then they may once again achieve normalcy, productivity, and happiness.

Finally, as a funeral director, I feel that the more caregivers can understand the varied hues of human existence and put this understanding to work in the service they perform, the more they will help those whom they serve and the greater fulfillment they will enjoy in the career they have designated as their life's work.

PARENTAL GRIEF AT THE DEATH OF AN ADULT CHILD INTERVIEW QUESTIONNAIRE

1. How old were you when the deceased died?

2. What was your marital status at the time?

3. How many years has it been since the death?

4. How old was the deceased?

5. What was the cause of death?

6. Do you have other children?

7. Have you had other deaths in your immediate family? Who?

8. How was this death different from others, if you have experienced other deaths? Or was it different?

9. What kind of initial reaction did you have when you first learned of it?

10. How did this death affect you? Loneliness? Alienation? Insecurity? Financial concerns? Emotional concerns?

11. Do you feel you have "gotten over" the death?

12. If so, what were the things that helped you in the short term? In the long term?

REFERENCES

Calhoun, L. G., Selby, J. W., and Steelman, J. K. 1983. *Individuals and Social Elements in Acute Grief: A Collection of Funeral Directors' Impressions of Suicidal Deaths*, as quoted in the *NS Mailgram*, December 29, 1983.

Cameron, N. 1963. *Personality Development and Psychopathology, A Dynamic Approach*. New York: Houghton Mifflin.

Droke, M. 1955. *The Christian Leaders' Golden Treasury*. New York: Grosset & Dunlap.

Fitzgerald, H.T. 1984. "Creating a Funeral for All the Family." *The American Funeral Director* (Jan.).

Jackson, E. N. 1957. *Understanding Grief*. Nashville, TN: Abingdon Press.

Kaplan, T. 1966. *Mr. Clemens and Mark Twain*. New York: Simon and Schuster.

Parkes, C. M. 1972. *Bereavement, Studies of Grief in Adult Life*. New York: International Universities Press.

Schiff, H. S. 1977. *The Bereaved Parent*. New York: Crown.

Steele, D. W. 1983. "The Bereaved Merit Special Attention." *Dodge Magazine* (Nov.).

Steele, D. W. 1984. "Hope in Grief." *Dodge Magazine* (Jan.).

6

Parental and Grandparental Grief for the Loss of an Adult Child

Robert G. Stevenson

The body of literature available to those of us who work with the bereaved has been augmented in the past decade by the addition of much valuable material. However, for those who work with bereaved parents who are attempting to cope with the loss of an adult child, there are still more questions than there are answers.

As an instructor of death education courses for well over a decade, I have found that the young people with whom I work fear old age more than death. They see children and grandchildren as the main source of solace in their old age. To face old age suddenly alone is unthinkable for them. It was in search of answers to their questions that I found that the questions outnumber the answers. Most of these questions can be combined into two large ones: What is the exact nature of the loss that has been suffered? How do the reactions of others affect the bereaved?

NATURE OF THE LOSS

In many ways, parents' reactions to the death of an adult child are the same as their reactions to the loss of any child. The first and strongest emotion they report is guilt, which comes from their having outlived their offspring. Because of this "offense" of surviving, many bereaved parents believe that they have been "bad parents." They see themselves as letting down their child and themselves. One often hears the questions, "Why me?" which means both "Why did this happen to me?" and "Why have I lived longer than my child?"

The death of an adult child is perceived as a violation of the natural order. However, its manifestations are internal and may not be readily apparent to those around the bereaved parents. If the parents saw their bid for personal immortality in their dead child, the loss is compounded. Therefore, not only must they mourn the loss of their child, they must mourn

51

the loss of that part of themselves that will no longer respond to the child. Older adults who are facing the loss of personal control over their lives see the death of an adult child as being yet another situation over which they have no control.

If one applies the general knowledge of the grief process to the experience of these individuals, two questions arise that warrant additional study. First, if grief produces feelings of helplessness and hopelessness, if the loss of an adult child causes feelings of worthlessness as a parent, and if the suicide rate is higher among senior citizens, might this population of older bereaved parents be at a higher risk of suicide?

Second, is the reaction to the loss of an adult child different for parents and grandparents? If the presence of an older sibling of the same sex as the deceased parent can help a bereaved child cope with the loss of parents, might there be a similar mechanism at work (in reverse) for grandparents or parents?

HOW DO OTHERS' REACTIONS AFFECT THE BEREAVED?

In many cases, the immediate circumstances of the bereaved remain unchanged. This lack of change may provide stability, but it can also be a constant contradiction of the internal feelings that are fully involved in the changes brought about by the loss. The friends who make up the parents' support network may have known the child only indirectly or not at all. Thus, they are hampered in their ability to provide effective support to the bereaved parents.

As older adults become increasingly isolated, the death of an adult child and the lack of an effective support network can make their isolation worse. In addition, the lack of visible change in the bereaved's immediate surroundings may cause some friends and relatives to relate to them as if no loss had occurred. The lack of acknowledgement of the bereaved parent's loss of an adult child and the negative effects of this lack of support are similar to what many husbands and wives experience after a miscarriage.

Platitudes fail with older bereaved parents. If one attempts to say that the deceased "lived a full life," what of the surviving parent? If the child's life was full, how can the older parent find continued meaning in his or her own life?

After witnessing several attempts to set policies for dealing with cases of this type of bereavement, chiefly in nursing homes and senior residences, I have come to see one rule that benefits the bereaved; that is, *acknowledge the loss.* Allow rituals to be held, encourage expressions of sorrow, admit that for the bereaved, something has changed, even if one has difficulty seeing exactly how.

In many ways, the reactions of these bereaved parents who have lost adult children are the same as those of any bereaved parents. The differences that we see may well come from our different reactions. Perhaps, after all, when we examine these unanswered questions, we should look first to ourselves. It is there that the answers lie.

7

Levels of Care of the Bereaved: Parental and Grandparental Grief for Loss of an Adult Child

Eric C. Keyser

Effective care of the bereaved begins with an understanding of interpersonal relationships and the use of basic counseling techniques to facilitate the grieving process. The funeral director should not be a sympathetic order taker, but an empathic, involved individual concerned with the emotional well-being of the bereaved.

The mode of the funeral is not the issue; it is simply a tool to be used to assist the bereaved. The funeral is a human relations experience. Its meaning and content must be reflective of the mores and values of the bereaved.

In our increasingly mobile and impersonal society, the need for skilled individuals is paramount. Too often the attitude is that what worked well yesterday is good enough today and even tomorrow. It is our job to create an atmosphere that promotes the therapeutic ventilation of grief in a natural manner. To oversimplify, individuals can begin to manifest their grief in normal channels. Conversely, they may bottle up their emotions and eventually have a "blowout." Many funeral directors would argue that it is neither their role nor their responsibility to become truly involved with the bereaved. They view their primary function as facilitators and expeditors who provide merchandise, facilities, and equipment. Anything else is left to other caregivers.

Too often, funeral directors fall into the rut of going through the motions and fail to

1. hear what is being said;
2. understand the bereaved's expressed needs;
3. help the bereaved ventilate their emotions;
4. establish an empathic relationship with the bereaved;
5. help create a meaningful service.

To establish an effective interview, one should be adept in the use of basic counseling techniques, which allow extreme flexibility in the majority of crisis situations that necessitate the involvement of a funeral director. The learning of these techniques takes a degree of formal study as well as basic sensitivity and an awareness of human nature. Most of these techniques and skills, many of which are derived from the Rogerian school of psychotherapy, are supportive but nondirective. It should be noted that these techniques are used only to facilitate understanding and communication, and to develop a meaningful funeral experience. These techniques are not used to analyze any individual or group.

To begin an effective relationship, it is necessary for the interviewer and the client to understand each other accurately. To develop this relationship, certain skills must be learned, practiced, and refined. There are four fundamental areas that need to be understood. The first is called *positive self-regard* (*congruence*). To achieve congruence, one must get in touch with one's true self and accept one's own feelings and attitudes. Only then will one be able and willing to take risks in the interview and to express oneself when it is appropriate to do so to develop a productive and helping relationship.

Second, the interviewer should have unconditional positive regard for the bereaved. When this is achieved, the interviewer experiences a warm, positive, accepting attitude toward the client. The interviewer cares for the client in a total, rather than a conditional, manner. It is an outgoing, positive, but nonevaluative approach. The interviewer accepts the client whether he or she agrees or disagrees with what is expressed during the interview.

Third, there is "phenomenological knowledge," that comes somewhere between subjective and objective knowing. This way of knowing employs the use of empathy, which is directed toward the individual during the interview. Finally, there is trust, without which the value of the experience is negated. These skill areas are developed by the use and understanding of the following techniques.

Self disclosures are a reporting of one's own feelings at a given time. The feelings are generally descriptions, and often are nonverbal. A feeling becomes a physical reaction to a thought. Self disclosures must be pertinent to the issue at hand; it is not what the interviewer thinks is important but what is important to the person being counseled. Active listening responses are nonevaluative methods of saying back to the individual the meanings the words have for oneself—in other words, it is paraphrasing. Paraphrasing is extremely important but, by the same token, care should be taken to avoid becoming preoccupied with interpreting what is being said. Paraphrasing crystallizes communication by reflecting back to the client what has been said. It allows one to check the meaning of the sentence. It is often helpful to preface one's response with, "It sounds like," "I hear you saying," or other such statements.

Paraphrasing encourages dialogue, builds trust, demonstrates the interviewer's interest in the client, and helps the client to feel understood. It aids the interviewer to see things from the other's perspective. Paraphrasing helps one's ability to hear, enabling one to listen acutely to what is being said. Listening, which is probably the most difficult skill to learn, is one of the most important and productive tools that interviewers can master. It requires that one not be preoccupied and involves hearing the way things are being said through the tones, expressions, and gestures used. Also, listening means looking for what is not being said, for what is being held back. It is important to follow the client's words and mannerisms as they are being used, thus engaging one's own thought processes before speaking. Although we hear with our ears, we must also listen with our eyes, mind, and heart.

Empathy is participating in another's feelings and putting oneself in another's situation. Empathetic interviewers attempt to get in touch with their client's internal frame of reference, to perceive each client's world as if it was their own. The "as if" is paramount to the relationship: if interviewers lose sight of their own selves, they can slip into identification with clients. This danger arises because interviewers cannot remain objective. They lose the intangible ability to use their own internal frames of reference, thus handicapping the interaction with the client.

Silence, when used by interviewers, can be highly effective. It gives the bereaved a chance to sort things out and continue. Interviewers can also use silence to consolidate their own thoughts, before continuing. The use of open-ended questions creates a vast realm of answers that include views, opinions, thoughts, and feelings. These questions, which should be indirect, allow the bereaved a full scope and help them to widen their perceptual field.

Feedback establishes the accuracy that clients understand. Without two-way exchange, interviewers are not able to gauge the effectiveness of an interview, thus lessening its effectiveness and creating misunderstanding during and after the interview.

The focus of this chapter has been to describe the use of effective communication and counseling techniques by funeral directors during their interactions with clients. Discussion of the techniques can be helpful whenever there are discussions of care for grandparents or parents who have experienced the death of an adult child.

How then do I begin an interview? It begins where the bereaved person is, with the anxieties he or she expresses. The interviewer must discard all old forms and methods and get on that emotional roller coaster with the bereaved. Open the interview with an open-ended, nondirective statement such as, "It must have been a shock," or "You've been anticipating this for quite a while." Then let the responses come. Forget about gathering all of the statistical information at this time; that will evolve during the course of the interview.

If you are talking with the parents or grandparents of a deceased child, they will often express their sorrow that the child died before them. One question is always asked: Why? They, the bereaved, have had a full life. Why did their loved one have to die first, why not them? The deceased child had so much to live for; so much was planned. Maybe the deceased left a husband, wife, or child, with so much more still to do. When an adolescent or young child dies, parents or grandparents often express a sense of guilt: if only they had done this, seen that doctor, or picked up the child instead of letting it walk. In each situation, the remorse often focuses on unexpressed love or unfulfilled dreams. The hurt is more for what might have been than for what had happened. There are always the "what ifs" and the "if onlys," all those sins of omission and commission that arise to haunt the bereaved. The hurt is real.

Forget about being in an uncomfortable situation and think back for a minute—generally, when you've been in an uncomfortable situation, it has been a learning and growing experience. So should the time spent with the bereaved be.

How does one continue? Let the bereaved express themselves. Continue exploring issues such as the cause of death, the length of illness, the treatment history, and who was aware or unaware of the condition. Did the family or the deceased talk openly about death? Did anyone talk openly with the deceased? What was most difficult to discuss? Were there matters the clients wish they had discussed but did not? Were important things talked about, and was this helpful? The most important thing a funeral director can do is help the family remember the facts—accurately. The one thing that is always said or implied to the funeral director, but that generally is not heard, is "I want to remember him as I knew him."

During this time, you will be gathering a wealth of information about such things as the deceased's religion, friends, affiliations, work, values, hobbies, likes, and dislikes. Using all of this information, it is possible to generate a meaningful service. Suggest alternatives, changes, participation. Too often, the funeral service is cast in concrete. It is thought that things must be done according to a certain form or protocol. You must convey this message to the bereaved. If something is important to them, then they should do it.

In conclusion, the challenge has never been greater. Those experiencing the death of a loved one are going through the most traumatic time in their lives. It is imperative to reach out and help. Only in this way will we be able to give fully of our time and talents in the grief continuum.

8

Bereavement and the Elderly: An Adult Child Dies

David E. Sanders

"I hate her." These are the words of a 72-year-old woman whose son had died of leukemia. Her bitter emotions are directed at her son's widow.

The grieving process takes many forms, and can be as varied as the diversity of human personalities. Studies have shown that the death of a child is perceived as the most painful event a person can encounter (Eissler 1971). To date, studies of parental bereavement have focused on the death of a child and its effects on the parents and the family in the context of childhood and adolescence, but not later in life. The aim of this chapter is to present some preliminary observations, by way of a case study, on the grief of elderly parents facing the death of their adult child.

Contrary to popular knowledge, it seems that the elderly fear death less than their young. There are those who contend that this relationship also exists regarding grief. Eissler has conjectured that "a reduction of the capacity to mourn occurs with fair regularity in the seventh decade. . . . Every human being eventually would reach the point, if he lived long enough, at which the ability to mourn would subside" (p. 99).

Compare Eissler's view to the following statement of a bereaved parent. "It does not appear to make a difference whether one's child is three, thirteen, or thirty, if he dies. The emotion in each of us is the same" (Schiff 1978:4). Gorer carries this view further. He feels that "the most distressing and long-lasting of all griefs, is that for the loss of a grown child. In such a case it seems to be literally true and not a figure of speech that the parents never get over it" (Gorer 1965). The resilient shell of the elderly in facing loss, postulated by Eissler, seems to shatter with the death of a child.

Presented in this chapter are segments of three interviews with an elderly couple, two years after the death of their 32-year-old son from leukemia. The father (Mr. P) was 80, his wife (Mrs. P) was 72. Much of their grief was still not resolved.

Mr. and Mrs. P's first two children were born during the early years of their marriage. The third and last child, Mr. P, Jr., was born almost a decade after the birth of their second child. The "baby" of the family lived alone with his parents more than ten years after his siblings had married. He married when he was 19, an age which his parents considered much too young. He died also at an age that his parents considered much too young.

Although this young man was diagnosed as having leukemia seven years prior to his death, he had had a number of extended remissions. His sickness had been concealed from his parents. Mr. P, Jr. confided in his older siblings, but swore them to secrecy. The deception continued until a week before his death, when Mr. P, Jr.'s condition had so worsened that it was deemed necessary to let the elderly parents know of their son's illness.

A segment of one of the interviews focused on some personal feelings at the time of their son's death.

Int: Your son had decided not to tell you of his illness for all those years. How did you feel about that?

Mrs. P: If we had known, his father would have fasted.

Mr. P: We would have prayed. Praying might have helped.

Mrs. P: But it wouldn't have helped for us to know. We are older people and we would have gotten sicker and sicker.

Int: Tell me a little about the week you spent with your son before he died?

Mrs. P: It was very good that we were there. When we went to visit him in the hospital, we felt very welcomed by him. He wasn't so friendly when other people came to visit. When Mr. P came in, he even sat up in his bed. He was having problems eating but he got much better. We left because he went home from the hospital.

Int: You left that week?

Mrs. P: We left before the weekend and were hoping to come back. He died that Friday night. She [the daughter-in-law] sent him back to the hospital that Friday night. He begged to stay home, but she sent him back. He hated the hospital, he wanted to die at home.

The second segment is taken from an interview conducted after Mr. and Mrs. P were informed that their daughter-in-law was planning to remarry. Their son had had three children before he died and the question of adoption was the focal point of the discussion. The children were 12, 10, and 5 years old at the time of the interview.

Int: Why do you dislike your daughter-in-law so much?

Mrs. P: I'll tell you about her. She is a selfish, spoiled creature. She didn't consider her husband.

Mr. P: She's a devil.

Mrs. P: She killed him. [Mr. P nodding approval.] She let him work hard, work nights, so that he could buy more and more insurance. As soon as he died she started fixing the house, she bought new furniture. . . . She didn't grieve when he died. She is already going to get married.

Int: Is she a good mother?

Mrs. P: She is good to the children. She loves them.

Mr. P: He [the new husband] should not adopt them. It's a financial matter.

Mrs. P: Well, she won't have them adopted because of all the money, the social security. That's what she is interested in, money.

Mr. P: If they are adopted, if they change their name I will not put them in my will. If they are adopted, our son will have lived in vain.

Mrs. P: They try to tell us that the daughter [the 12 year old] will change her name anyway when she gets married. But, when they are adopted, they won't know about their father anymore. I don't think they'll change their name anyway because of the money and that's all she is interested in.

Mr. P: If I didn't have to worry about the adopting, it would be a load off my mind. If she gets married again, I won't go into the house [tears] . . .

The third and final segment is from an interview conducted a year later. Mr. P, who had greater difficulty dealing with his grief than his wife, appeared to have achieved some resolution of his grief. It would seem that for him the greatest therapeutic tool was the passage of time.

Int: Mr. P, how do you feel?

Mr. P: If she [his wife] feels bad, I feel bad. If she feels good, I feel good.

Int: I haven't seen you smile before today?

Mr. P: You see, if I cry, it makes her sick. I want her to be well. I vowed I wouldn't cry anymore.

Int: How have you resolved your grief?

Mr. P: My doctor said to me that I can't go on like this. I have to start living again and stop grieving. What can I do? I just bend my head and accept it.

Int: What about visiting your grandchildren?

Mr. P: I won't go into the house!

Mrs. P: [Interrupting] But darling, you are going to have to visit them.

The scars still remain, or as Gorer put it, "the parents never get over it" (Gorer 1965: 121). Yet, Mr. and Mrs. P were on their way toward a healthy adjustment.

The following sections discuss guilt feelings and the grieving process, using the case report as an illustration.

GUILT

Bereaved parents commonly say that they wish they had died instead of their child. To elaborate, they explain that they had lived a full life, that their child was so young and had a long life to look forward to. Mr. and Mrs. P also expressed this desire. However, this attitude does not imply that the parents have necessarily come to a great acceptance of their own death.

The fact that Mr. P, Jr. had concealed his illness from his parents may have contributed significantly to their feelings of guilt. They had been denied the opportunity to share in caring for their son, and in the sharing of feelings and thoughts. Also of significance is that Mr. and Mrs. P might have misinterpreted their son's charades and continuous excuses; finding out the true reason behind his behavior may have made them feel guilty for having misjudged their son. Mr. and Mrs. P seemed to have accepted their son's decision not to inform them of his sickness, yet this did not preclude feelings of guilt. This guilt may be channeled into anger against their other children who participated in the conspiracy of silence.

When guilt becomes too difficult to integrate, it is often displaced and converted into anger. This is especially so if certain ambivalent feelings toward the deceased were not allowed to surface.

The ambivalence which is a natural constituent of the
parent's feelings toward a child, but ordinarily repressed,
becomes a strong and sometimes crazed accuser which
demands retribution. In certain instances a parent
sees this presumed hostile intent toward the deceased
child in the spouse or in an older child who is held
responsible and furiously assailed for the fantasied
death dealing intent. (Halpern 1979)

Mr. and Mrs. P indeed accused their daughter-in-law of "kill-
ing" their son, by "forcing" him to work hard for her benefit
and by sending him back to the hospital against his wishes.
It is important to clarify areas of speculation and remove fantasy from fact in order to facilitate better communication and
to break down barriers that block the grieving process.

GRIEF

As we have pointed out, the death of a child is the "ultimate tragedy." This may be more clearly understood by realiz-
ing that "the child is an extension of self in space and time.
With death, both aspects of the parent are cut off. As long
as the offspring lives, the parent's awareness of personal mortality is attenuated if not suppressed. The loss of this cover
of one's own finite existence registers alarm, fear and hopelessness" (Halpern 1979). These observations, as well as the
following consideration, are certainly valid regarding the
elderly. "When the child has carried additional parental hopes,
for example that he or she become someone who the parent
could not be, then the unfulfilled longings are doubly thwarted
by the death" (Halpern 1979). For Mr. and Mrs. P, the situation was slightly brightened because they could still look with
pleasure to the future lives of their other children and their
families. If the child who dies is an only child, the situation
becomes potentially more acute, and the relationship of grandparent to grandchildren (when present) becomes more crucial,
as the extension of self is perceived through the grandchildren.
We saw that Mr. and Mrs. P's relationship with their
daughter-in-law was hostile. Silverman, in discussing the tension between parents and widow, suggests that

they may be a result of some parents' inability to find
a way of expressing their grief, and of accommodating
to it. They are angry and experience great resentment
when they see that the widow can rebuild her life.
While she may not necessarily remarry, she knows
what she lost, what is missing from her life, and what
she must now live without. It is more difficult to
rationally explain what it means to lose a child.
(Silverman 1977:11)

Mr. and Mrs. P's resentment can be seen from the following statements. "As soon as he died she started fixing the house, she bought new furniture [showing the ability to rebuild her life]. . . . She didn't grieve when he died. She is already going to get married."

Often, though, there is much affection and the in-laws may find it comforting to become involved with the bereaved spouse's problems. As parents who have a child after the death of another child learn that this can have an assuaging effect on the sorrow and emptiness through the potential of cathexis to another living being, the elderly can invest and direct their energies to the surviving spouse and the grandchildren.

When elderly parents are not allowed to share in the knowledge of their child's illness, they are deprived of the opportunity to work out past conflicts and part on peaceful terms, to express love (a last time), and to feel a sense of self-worth. They are also deprived of a period of anticipatory grief. As Lindemann has pointed out, "anticipatory grief may well form a safeguard against the impact of a sudden death notice" (Lindemann 1944:148). Mr. and Mrs. P were told of their son's illness only a week before his death, a period too short to permit them to assimilate the seriousness of the situation.

On the other hand, the siblings and other family members had been processing the anticipated death of Mr. P, Jr. for seven years. Although Feifel (1979) has likened this situation to "ships passing in the fog," it may be better described as "ships colliding in the fog." Family and staff members must become sensitive to this imbalance, and realize that the elderly parent in this situation may require a greater degree of attention and communication.

CONCLUSION

While we have attempted to discuss a topic that has not received much attention in the literature, it seems evident that with the ever-increasing elderly population, continued investigations into thanatological issues involving the elderly are of importance. Although elderly parents may react in ways that are similar to their younger counterparts, there are likely to be important differences.

As an epilogue to this chapter, it is rewarding to report that Mr. and Mrs. P have visited their newly married "daughter-in-law" and had dinner with the new family. The flexibility of the elderly should never be underestimated.

REFERENCES

Eissler, K. 1971. *Talent and Genius*. New York: Quadrangle
 Books.

Feifel, H. 1979. "Death and Loss in Modern America." Keynote
 address, Sixth Annual Conference on Bereavement and
 Grief, Yeshiva University, New York.

Gorer, G. 1965. *Death, Grief and Mourning*. New York: Anchor
 Books, Doubleday.

Halpern, W. I. 1979. "Parental Mortification and Restitutional
 Efforts Upon the Sudden Loss of a Child." Paper presented
 at the Symposium on the Child and Death, the Foundation
 of Thanatology, Columbia Presbyterian Medical Center,
 New York.

Lindemann, E. 1944. "Symptomatology and Management of
 Acute Grief." *American Journal of Psychiatry* 101:141–148.

Schiff, H. S. 1978. *The Bereaved Parent*. New York: Penguin
 Books.

Silverman, P. R. 1977. "General Aspects." In N. Linser, ed.,
 Understanding Bereavement and Grief. New York: Yeshiva
 University Press.

9

One Parent's Experience with the Death of an Adult Child

Frances Karlan

A simple question that is asked innumerable times and rarely creates any problem is "How many children do you have?" Three years have passed since my daughter's death, but I have not yet learned to cope with this question. My husband's answer is likely to be, "We had two" or "One, now." Each of these answers, of course, opens up a discussion that I would be more comfortable avoiding. My husband has not yet learned to say, "We have a son." I am not sure I can do it either. When I am with a new group of people and the subject arises, I tend to shudder. I dread it. Sometimes I walk out of the room, but if I am forced to answer, I am determined to say "one"; however, even if I do, the hurt is overwhelming, and sometimes I walk out of the room after I have said it. Afterwards, all the hurt starts over again. I hope that both of us will learn to cope with a question like this in time.

The death of a child is different for each parent, depending on the age of the deceased child and the ages of the bereaved parents, which will determine whether replacement is possible. The response to the death of a child is also affected by the attitudes of friends, relatives, and surviving children; the number and sex of the surviving children; the parents' work environments and religious preferences; the support the spouses give each other; the presence of grandchildren; the parents' relationship with the deceased child; and the nature of the death—whether it was accidental or prolonged.

The manifestations of grief also vary with different people, depending on their upbringing. For example, in my religion, Judaism, it is customary to send a "tree certificate," which indicates that a tree has been planted in Israel in the name of the deceased person. We must have received hundreds of these certificates in our daughter's name. When I happened to drive by a forest that was dedicated to someone, I became hysterical. When my husband asked why I was crying, I said, "I have a pile of these certificates, but I don't have her." Grief seems to surface at odd times and no matter how much control one has.

Our daughter was 32 years old, married, and a successful lawyer. She was well adjusted and outgoing, loved life and living, and had the means to live the way she wished. Her last words to me two days before she died were, "Mom, if I have a baby, will you help me?" I can only thank heaven that I did say yes at that point because I used to tell her jokingly, "With me you don't have a baby sitter." Her death was an accident; it was sudden. Her husband was driving the car; the car skidded and they smashed into an embankment. He walked out of the car unhurt, but she was killed instantly. Of course, even though we realized that he was not at fault, his driving and surviving unhurt have caused us to have conflicting feelings toward him, which we have tried to control.

My immediate reactions to our daughter's death were shock and disbelief—the feeling that it was just a bad dream from which I would wake up. I do not remember being in shock; I can only suppose I was because people told me that I looked different. I remember that I felt despair right after the funeral. In my desperation, I said to one of my daughter's friends who is a psychiatrist, "Steve, help me!" He answered, "I can't help you. Your problems are real, they are not for a psychiatrist."

When she died, we looked at the body; my husband cried but I did not. I cried only when I was alone, never when anyone could see me. My inability to cry was a part of my Germanic, New England upbringing. During my childhood, my father repeatedly said to me, "Don't cry; don't ever let anyone see you cry." This was my conditioning. I saw my parents bury my sister. Although I know they felt grief, they did not shed a tear. Tears are no indication of internal emotion.

We drove home the night of our daughter's death and stopped to have a bite to eat. The next morning, we packed to stay at our daughter's and son-in-law's house to make plans for the funeral. While we were at their house, everything reminded us of her. Photographs were a torment; I could not look at pictures of her. Nevertheless, we did what had to be done. We were in full control of our senses. We sought solace from one another when we were alone. Our only relief, our only comfort, was from each other. I think that instinctively we were trying to spare other people embarrassment because they did not know how to handle her death.

If you want to advise people how to respond to their friends' bereavement, tell them not to be afraid to talk—to say they are sorry and to talk about the deceased. Bereaved parents want to talk. Some of my oldest, closest friends have not been in touch with me since my daughter's death. Others avoided me for a long time, as if I was a leper whose bereavement was a contagious disease.

As a result of the reactions of friends, many bereaved parents turn to others in the same predicament and build close relationships with them that are based on an understanding of how to deal with the intense grief over such an unnatural event as the death of one's child. For example, on my first day back at work about a week after my daughter died, I parked my car and was standing at the corner waiting to cross the street. I am sure that my stance must have conveyed my feelings. Suddenly, there was a hand on my shoulder, and a male voice said, "Come, we will cross together. I know how you feel. Let me help you." He said nothing more, but he did not have to. My colleague had lost a son two months earlier. He has been a source of never-ending strength and comfort over the past three years.

After the first shock wore off, my husband and I tried to resume normal living. That is not really possible, but one does go on with the outward trappings. I only wanted to be with people I felt understood my problem. Because most people did not, I withdrew into myself. I avoided family gatherings. I dreaded weddings, festive affairs, and holidays. To this day, we have not celebrated birthdays, anniversaries, or any other events that remind us of better times. My daughter's birthday was in November, and her favorite holiday was Thanksgiving. Therefore, November has become a nightmare to us. I stopped sending Christmas cards; the words "Happy New Year" had become a mockery. One understanding close friend who visited us on New Year's Day said, "I hope it is a better year than the previous one." Her response meant so much. She could not wish us a happy holiday, but she could understand our suffering and express it. Although our grief surfaced, it would have surfaced anyway.

Some people think that bereaved parents are prone to physical illness. Although I came down with the flu about a month after our daughter's death, I cannot say that I got the flu because I was bereaved and hence was more susceptible. It was February and the flu was going around; maybe I would have gotten it anyway. A year later, my husband had an acute gall bladder attack. I do not believe that his bereavement caused the gallstones to be caught in the common bile duct even though there are people who might say that this is the sort of thing that can happen. However, I do know that while my husband was in the hospital, he reacted terribly—with the surgeon, me, and everyone. But I suspect that he did so partly because he could not cope emotionally with the fact that our son-in-law had remarried that week.

In the case of the bereaved family, another problem, of course, is the reactions of siblings. I am experienced with this problem not only because I am a bereaved parent who has a surviving son, but because when my sister died I saw my parents in the same predicament and I suddenly became an only child. This is exactly what happened to my son. He has had great difficulty coping with the fact that now he is the only one who is "responsible" for us. My husband and I have noticed a phenomenon that tends to frighten us: We worry about him. If he is driving the car, traveling in an airplane, or just happens not to call us for a week, we tend to panic. Then my common sense tells me, "Stop it, he will be all right." But, I say to myself, "Well, my luck did not hold out once; I am not sure it will this time." There is no way that a person who has not been through this experience can possibly understand the pain, the frustration, the loneliness, the longing, the anger, and the disbelief that such a terrible thing could happen. To this day, I tend to fantasize. I close my eyes and think that when I open them I will hear her footsteps and I will see her coming toward me. This is a common reaction.

I found—as have all my friends who have lost children—that the second year was as bad as the first year because reality set in. The finality of my daughter's death finally reached consciousness. It is particularly difficult when the deceased child is an adult because replacement is not possible. Also, the parents are generally older, and their resilience and ability to cope are diminished. There is no future, there is only the past. During the second year, I still did not seek people out. I still did not like nor could I enjoy festive affairs, particularly family ones of which my daughter would have been a part. I tended to think that other people do not appreciate their children enough—that one appreciates people much more when one cannot be with them. However, we still took part in gatherings and meetings, we laughed and sang, went to movies and plays.

Toward the end of the second year and into the third, we maintained all the outward trappings of a full life because we had to. One cannot become a recluse; that is not the answer. We have a son who loves us, who hurts with us, and who must lead a normal life. Therefore, our grief is ours alone, hidden from the public, surfacing daily, and still having enough intensity to hurt, but under control.

Now we are in our third year, and I notice an awakening of certain emotions. It is just a stirring, but I am beginning to think—and this is the first time I have done so—that summer is coming; maybe a trip to Montreal would be nice, or perhaps Toronto. We have family in both cities. It is time.

10

The Bereaved Parents of Adult Children: A Case for Study

I. Levav, M. Lubner, and I. Adler

INTRODUCTION

Although bereavement is a universal experience, most of us
are spared a certain type of loss, the death of a child. The
effect of this loss has been reckoned as "the most significant
and traumatic event a person is likely to experience" (Gorer
1965). Gorer implicitly separates out the effects of bereavement
by the age of the offspring. He suggests that "the most distressing and long lasting of all grief . . . is the loss of a
grown child," perhaps because such a loss cannot be accepted
as "part of the natural order of universal dynamics" (Sanders
1979-80). Indeed, as Palgi (1973) wrote, "societies regard the
death of people in their prime or on the threshold of life as
a violation of the laws of nature, so much so, that death rituals are usually bound up with the concept of respect for
one's elders."

Considering the intense and prolonged suffering that seems
to be associated with such bereavement, it is surprising to
note that the loss of an adult child remains a virtually neglected subject in bereavement research. It rather quickly becomes apparent to the reviewer that the field of adult bereavement has developed asymmetrically: The greater amount of
work has centered on conjugal bereavement. Such asymmetry
has led Sanders (1979-80) to conclude that bereavement research "has focused (almost exclusively) on the problems en-
countered following the death of a spouse." The few studies
of parental bereavement have often been limited in scope or
have been included as a secondary part of a larger study
(see below). Some of the limitations have arisen from the

We thank Dr. B. P. Dohrenwend for his critique of an
early review of the draft and Drs. B. S. Dohrenwend, S. L.
Kark, and E. Peritz for contributions made to the development
of the paper.

investigator's failure to examine the effects of the loss over a sufficiently long period. Other studies have been hampered by the types of measures employed. Most frequently, the studies of parental bereavement have been limited by the use of a particularly small sample. For instance, Gorer's (1965) widely quoted statement above was made after interviews with only six people who had lost a child during the previous three years.

Despite the paucity of research in this area, the first question that arises is what direct or indirect evidence can be extracted from the literature to provide us with some knowledge of the effects of the death of a grown child on the surviving parents. This in turn generates another question as to whether or not this kind of bereavement constitutes a public health problem that is deserving of further investigation. As Kark (1974) would ask, what is the "case for study"?

This chapter is an attempt to review, in part, the available research evidence in the area of parental bereavement. Following the authors' research interests, two particular aspects, parental mortality and psychopathology, will be examined. Most of the articles selected for this discussion are epidemiological in nature. They have been selected because they are more suited to the objective of this paper and because they tend to use larger samples and better controls than do the clinical studies.

PARENTAL BEREAVEMENT AND MORTALITY

An understanding of the effects of parental bereavement on mortality can be gained by examining the data to ascertain:

1. whether or not there is an elevated risk of mortality among surviving relatives in general;
2. whether or not bereaved parents are a subgroup of surviving relatives who are at great risk for mortality; and
3. whether or not any relevant knowledge about parents can be gained from the examination of other, similar subgroups of surviving relatives.

In this manner, all available evidence on bereaved relatives can be used to estimate the magnitude of the risk of mortality among parents who have lost a grown child.

Evidence for the first issue, higher risk of mortality among bereaved relatives, is readily available. Three rather recent reviews (Clayton 1974; Jacobs and Ostfeld 1977; Klerman and Izen 1977) have been published on the association between the loss of a loved one and mortality. The original studies critically reviewed in these papers are epidemiological in type and used either retrospective or prospective designs. Although their methods and procedures were not entirely free of flaws,

the studies reviewed are solid enough to allow conclusions to
be drawn from them. The interested reader is referred to
those reviews. However, it is sufficient to indicate here that
with the exceptions of Clayton 1974, Gerber et al. 1975, and
Ward 1976, these studies indicate that there is an elevated risk
of death among the bereaved (Table 10.1). Many of these differences in results can be accounted for by the methodological
difficulties present in all such studies. These problems range
from possible misstatements and incomplete information on the
death certificates used in retrospective studies to unrepresen-
tative sampling, incomplete participation, small sample size, and
lack of appropriate controls or other comparison groups—more
common difficulties in prospective studies (Jacobs and Ostfeld
1977). Nevertheless, it does seem that "despite methodologic
bias and limitations, the perspective of 17 years of varied
methodology and the repetition of findings enhance the substance of the basic association between conjugal bereavement
and elevated risk of death" (Jacobs and Ostfeld 1977).

The greatest risk of mortality is present during the first
24 months after the loss, regardless of the cause of death or
the sex of the bereaved. More precisely, the risk for men is
highest during the first six months. However, Parkes, Benjamin, and Fitzgerald (1969) found that among their widowed
subjects, the increased mortality rate remained high until the
end of the fourth year of bereavement. Similarly, for the surviving spouses of suicides, the relative risk stays higher
until the fourth year (McMahon and Pugh 1965). It seems,
then, that surviving relatives in general do have an elevated
risk of mortality. However, the studies mentioned above refer
almost exclusively to conjugal bereavement. Is there any
similar evidence concerning bereaved parents?

The answer was indicated earlier: almost none. Only one
study (Rees and Lutkins 1967) included parents among the
survivors. The authors investigated the death rates of the
close relatives of 371 residents of a semirural area of Wales
who died between January 1, 1960 and December 31, 1965.
Among the 903 surviving relatives, there were 35 parents,
who were matched with 29 parents of the 878 relatives making
up the control group. The reading of Rees and Lutkins's (1967)
study would leave the mistaken impression that there is no
elevated risk for the bereaved parents. In a table displaying
the statistical significance of the difference in mortality recorded during the first year of bereavement for the different
groups of survivors (all relatives, parents, the widowed,
children, siblings), the bereaved parents do not appear to
differ significantly from the controls in their risk of mortality.
A different result is obtained, however, when the accumulated
deaths of the bereaved parents are compared with those of
the controls for a period of five years. Our recalculations are
shown in Table 10.2. Since the bereaved parents do not seem
to have been an unduly old group—although this is not speci-

TABLE 10.1 Mortality of Bereavement—Summary of Nine Studies

Study	I	II	III	IV	V*	VI	VII	VIII	IX
Author/s	Kraus & Lilienfeld	Young, Benjamin & Wallis	Cox & Ford	Rees & Lutkins	Parkes, Benjamin & Fitzgerald	McNeill	Clayton	Gerber et al.	Ward
Year	1959	1963	1964	1967	1969	1973	1974	1975	1976
Country	USA	U.K.	U.K.	U.K.	U.K.	USA	USA	USA	U.K.
Source of	Vital statistics	Vital statistics	Vital statistics	Cohort	Vital statistics	Vital statistics	Cohort	Cohort	Cohort
Bereaved	Spouses	Spouses	Spouses	Close relatives	Spouses	Spouses	Spouses	Spouses	Spouses
Risk for Mortality	Elevated	Elevated	Elevated	Elevated	Elevated	Elevated	Unchanged	Unchanged	Unchanged

*Parkes, Benjamin, and Fitzgerald (1969) followed the same population of bereaved as Young, Benjamin, and Wallis (1963) into the fifth year.
Source: Authors.

TABLE 10.2   Accumulated Deaths of Bereaved Parents and Controls over Five Years (Recalculated from Rees and Lutkins, 1967)

	Total (N)	Deaths		Alive	
		Number	Percent	Number	Percent
Bereaved parents	35	12	34.3	27	65.7
Control parents	29	2	6.9	29	93.1

x^2 = 8.64; d.f. = 1; p < .01.
Source: Authors.

fied in Rees and Lutkins's article—the difference in the percentage of deaths between the index and control groups is remarkable.

As mentioned above, given such a dearth of data on bereaved parents, one is forced to search the literature for some information on the risk of mortality among bereaved parents. This is done by examining the characteristics of those survivors who are in some ways similar to our target group.

One feature that surely characterizes the loss of an adult child or, for that matter, a child of any age, is that of untimeliness. Are there any indications that untimely deaths carry a risk (or perhaps, a greater risk) for the survivor? Indeed, some studies have implicitly considered this point when comparisons were made between the death rates of younger surviving spouses and older ones. It is expected that younger survivors would have suffered a more untimely loss than the older ones, and that this would be reflected in a greater risk of mortality among them. Kraus and Lilienfeld (1959), in a study that has become a classic in the epidemiological literature on this subject, found that for both white and nonwhite males and females, the risk of death was higher for those age 20 to 34 than for those age 35 to 44. They concluded that "the ratios for the widowed decrease steadily with increasing age." Rees and Lutkins (1967) found that "people who die following a bereavement are on the average slightly younger than the relatives who pre-deceased them, and they died at an earlier age than is usual for the community in which they live." Jacobs and Ostfeld (1977) reviewed additional studies in which younger widowed subjects had a higher risk than older ones. In short, it seems that the more untimely the death, the greater the risk for the survivor.

Besides untimeliness, bereaved parents of adult children experience a loss that is largely *unexpected*, since the causes of death are often conditions such as accidents (e.g., motor vehicle or work-related), self-inflicted injuries and, in a number of countries, war. In fact, what is known about unexpected death and its association with mortality rates? Intuitively, an association is expected. Rees and Lutkins (1967) confirmed this hunch: "If the primary death occurs at some site—for example a road or field—other than at home or hospital, the risk of a close relative dying during the first year of bereavement is five times the risk carried by the close relatives of people who die at home."

The concept of anticipatory grief is a complex one, however. The term is usually understood to be the grief process that a person goes through before the death of a significant other. It is usually believed that this process mitigates the grief reactions once the actual loss occurs. Conversely, unexpected and sudden death tends to be associated with more severe grief reactions and increased risk of mortality (Richards and McCullum 1979; Rees and Lutkins 1967; Jacobs and Ostfeld 1977; and Ball 1976, to mention a few). Not all investigators have found this to be the case, however (Ward 1976; Sanders 1979-80).

An issue that emerges from all of these studies concerns the appropriateness of the definitions of "short" or "long" illnesses, because it has not been established how much time is needed for anticipatory grief reactions to occur. Indeed, it is possible that very short illnesses do not allow enough time for the process of anticipatory grief to become established, whereas long illnesses may mean that the survivors become emotionally depleted and therefore are prone to intense grief reactions by the time the loss actually does occur. Another issue is that the relationship between the age of survivors and their grief reactions has not always been taken into account. The importance of this is indicated by Ball's (1976) study, in which she found that anticipatory grief had a stronger mitigating influence on the grief of widows under the age of 45, but that, in general, age was a more important factor in predicting the severity of the survivors' grief reactions than was mode of death.

Although the issue of anticipatory grief remains unclear, it does seem highly likely that untimely and unexpected losses carry a higher risk of mortality for the survivors. It is reasonable to expect that bereaved parents would fit into such a category too. However, further confirmation of their vulnerability is still required. One study (Rees and Lutkins 1967), which used a small number of subjects, did not provide direct evidence to support the hypothesis that bereaved parents are at greater risk of mortality. Although the indirect evidence appears to support the hypothesis, it can do no more than open this issue for discussion rather than bring it to a close.

PARENTAL BEREAVEMENT AND PSYCHOPATHOLOGY

The field of bereavement research was criticized by Klein (1972) as being anecdotal and devoid of rigorous data. It would hardly deserve such a description today, thanks to the contributions of authors such as Parkes, Clayton, Maddison, Viola, and others. As in the case of mortality (see above), the progress that has been made in this field is largely confined to conjugal bereavement. Unfortunately, studies on parental bereavement and psychopathology are still open to Klein's (1972) criticism, in that they have been conducted with a small number of subjects and without controls. Nevertheless, a few studies are available. One of them, by Sanders (1979-80), is most interesting because she compared grief reactions resulting from the loss of a spouse, child, or parent. In her study, 14 of the 102 survivors were parents (4 fathers and 10 mothers) whose ages ranged between 27 and 67 years (mean, 49.6); the ages of their dead children ranged between 6½ and 49 years. She studied the parents' reactions by means of a carefully designed grief inventory of acceptable internal reliability. Her findings were most clear: "Those who experienced the death of a child revealed more intense grief reactions in a number of scales, e.g., despair, somatization, anger, guilt than did those bereaved who had experienced the death of either a spouse or a parent." In general, "the death of a child produced the higher intensities of bereavement as well as the widest range of reactions." For the purposes of this chapter, Sanders's report unfortunately presents some difficulties: The exact number of children who died is not stated and a fine breakdown by age of child is not given, although their age range—10 to 14 years—is reported. Most important, there is no information on the duration of the parental grief reactions, since the interviews took place an average of 2.2 months after the loss.

One community study by two Israeli researchers, Purisman and Maoz (1977), was based on interviews of 47 parents from 25 families who had lost an adult son during the War of Attrition (1969-70). As far as we know, their study is the only one of its kind: never before or since have war-bereaved parents been studied. In fact, their study is the only one that deals exclusively with the effects of the death of adult children. The implications of this paper are manifold. Thus, despite its methodological shortcomings, it will be reviewed in some detail. Purisman and Moaz's interview included nine items that purported to measure a construct that the authors named "adjustment." These items were disturbed sleep, appetite, and weight loss; illness and deterioration in health; diverse complaints such as feeling unwell, headaches, difficulties in concentrating, feelings of guilt, expressions of blame, and changed social habits; changes in habits of relaxation; and work difficulties. The interviews, which took place two to three years after the loss, indicated that "the majority of bereaved parents changed their social habits [and] seldom went outside the front door." It is not clear from the study whether the individual items reported were the only ones in which parents were found to have problems at the time of the interview or whether they were indications of a prolonged and varied reaction, as manifested by all of the scale items. If this was the case, the parents' reactions would have had a longer duration than has been reported for widows (Clayton and Darvish 1979). Unfortunately, Purisman and Moaz's (1977) study suffers from methodological limitations, as the authors themselves have acknowledged. There was no control group; there was fuzziness about what was measured, in that their construct of "adjustment" seems to be a combination of selected items of psychopathology and role performance; and there was no attempt to check the reliability and validity of the scale (or scales). The conclusion to be drawn from this study is almost a truism: the important subject of war-related bereavement has been inadequately covered.

Schwab et al. (1975) reported a small community study of grief. Three of the bereaved relatives interviewed by the research team were biological parents and one was a surrogate parent. The latter was an aunt of the deceased. The interviews took place at two time points, the first within a year after the loss and the second a year later. The intensity of the grief reaction was measured by a scale based on the interviewers' ratings. The three scale categories were intense, moderate, and minimal grief reactions. At the time of the first interview, all four parents were found to be grieving intensely. The grief reactions of two of them remained unresolved by the time of the second interview. However, in view of the limited number of subjects studied, no valid conclusions can be drawn from this survey.

In contrast with the above studies, which used the community as a sampling frame, Paykel et al. (1969) relied on a patient population. Although the number of parents interviewed was small, this study yields additional information. The investigators compared the life events experienced by depressed patients and control subjects. A significant number of patients reported the death of an immediate family member during the six months preceding the onset of their disorder. Of these sixteen family members who had died, five were children.

In one study (Rahe 1975), 125 life events were assessed by community judges in the city of Jerusalem to determine the amount of readjustment that would be required if they were to be experienced. It was found that the death of a son in war, the death of a child as a result of unspecified circumstances, and the death of a spouse ranked higher, in that order, than all the other events. It seems that the ratings of these judges have been supported by the research evidence accumulated so far.

Since the direct research evidence is incomplete and meager, the same strategy followed for mortality, that is, that of using indirect evidence about other survivors, can be adopted to explore the association between parental bereavement and psychopathology. As mentioned earlier, the deaths of adult children are untimely and, most often, unexpected. Parkes' (1975) research on young Boston widowed people is helpful in this regard since it explores the effect of both features. He found that when death is unexpected, the outcome of the grief reaction is poorer and more long-lasting (at least four years, which was the limit of his research). At least one clinically based study concluded that "pathological reactions to death are more frequent when the death is untimely and sudden" (Lehrman 1956). However, this issue too is unresolved, since sudden death does not produce more disturbed survivors, at least not among the widowed. The potential pathogenic effect of the untimeliness of a loss on survivors has not yet been studied epidemiologically.

THE CASE FOR STUDY

Gorer (1965) wrote that "the loss of a child is against the order of nature. . . . The parents never get over it." This certainly seems to be borne out by the evidence presented earlier. And yet, data are lacking, even for a country such as Israel where there is high sensitivity to the subject of fallen soldiers and their bereaved families. Purisman and Maoz (1977) pointed out that "there is a large group of such parents in Israel and their problems are a painful and an ever-present aspect of Israeli life." However, the uniqueness of their study has already been mentioned.

Epidemiological research on bereavement and mortality has either excluded parents or included a small number of them (see Rees and Lutkins 1967), so that the findings are inconclusive. The subject requires investigation because it is highly likely that a profound effect does indeed exist. It can be hypothesized that the relative risk of mortality is high and that the effect of an untimely and unexpected loss strengthens the risk to the survivor.

It should not be overlooked that in addition to the preventive and social aspects that merit a case for study, the subject of parental bereavement, as it affects the risk for mortality, offers additional interest to researchers. The hypotheses formulated to interpret the association between bereavement and mortality are reduced to only two from the possible five in the case of conjugal bereavement. Klerman and Izen (1977) reviewed these five hypotheses. They are, with slight modifications, (1) hogogamy (assortive mating), (2) joint exposure to unfavorable environment, (3) common infection, (4) engagement in life-endangering behavior, and

(5) the desolation effect. The first three are not applicable in the special case of war-related parental bereavement. Since the number of hypotheses is narrowed down to only two, a research strategy could be used to explore the relative weight of the mechanism at stake. Such a study is feasible, particularly in a country like Israel, where parents have lost sons in war and where there are unusual facilities for epidemiological research.

Not less than for the association between parental bereavement and mortality, there is a case for study regarding psychiatric morbidity. The research evidence accrued so far, although far from complete, seems to indicate that grief among parents is very intense. According to Lehrman (1956), the reaction can reach pathological proportions, and is also quite likely to be prolonged. The latter characteristic requires additional research. For widows, it seems that the reaction is worsened when the loss is unexpected, especially when the widows' ages and, presumably, their stages of life are taken into account. However, this issue too remains unresolved. For instance, Bornstein et al. (1973) and Parkes (1975) have produced results that do not support this hypothesis. In the similar case of bereaved parents, Purisman and Maoz (1977) noted some possible effects two to three years after the loss. However, given the limitations of their study, no firm conclusions could be reached.

The death of adult children is rare, but it does occur. For societies that have suffered and still suffer from wars, whether internal or external, the importance of the subject is not a mere reflection of the number of deaths. It is perhaps more appropriate to measure the importance of this issue by the feeling that the losses were the heavy toll paid to assure the existence of a nation or of a type of society within it. This explains the nationally evoked concern for those most immediately affected: widows, orphans, and parents. In the absence of a remedy for wars, what else is left to reduce the impact of the tragedy?

To conclude, the case for study of the effects of bereavement on surviving parents, regarding their risk for both psychiatric morbidity and mortality, seems to be well grounded with respect to the current state of knowledge in the field. The research inquiry, however, could eventually move beyond the step of confirmation of the available findings and toward substantive issues, since bereavement constitutes a paradigm of an "experiment of nature" (Klerman and Izen 1977) on a powerful single social stressor (Cobb 1974) about which all is not yet known.

REFERENCES

Ball, J. F. 1976-1977. "Widow's Grief: The Impact of Age and Mode of Death." *Omega* 7(4): 307-333.

Bornstein, P. E., P. J. Clayton, J. A. Halikas, W. L. Maurice, and E. Robins. 1973. "The Depression of Widowhood After Thirteen Months." *British Journal of Psychiatry* 122: 561-566.

Clayton, P. J. 1974. "Mortality and Morbidity in the First Year of Widowhood." *Archives of General Psychiatry* 30: 747-750.

Clayton, P. J., and H. S. Darvish. 1979. "Course of Depressive Symptoms Following the Stress of Bereavement." In J. E. Barrett, R. M. Rose, and G. L. Klerman, eds. *Stress and Mental Disorder*. New York: Raven Press.

Cobb, S. 1974. "A Model for Life Events and Their Consequences." In B. S. Dohrenwend and B. P. Dohrenwend, eds. *Stressful Life Events: Their Nature and Effects*. New York: Wiley.

Gerber, I., R. Rusalem, N. Hannon, D. Battin, and A. Arkin. 1975. "Anticipatory Grief and Aged Widows and Widowers." *Journal of Gerontology* 30: 225-229.

Gorer, G. 1965. *Death, Grief and Mourning*. London: Cresset Press.

Jacobs, S., and A. Ostfeld. 1977. "An Epidemiological Review of the Mortality of Bereavement." *Psychosomatic Medicine* 34(5): 344-351.

Kark, S. L. 1974. *Epidemiology and Community Medicine*. New York: Appleton-Century-Crofts.

Klein, D. F. 1972. "Methodology for Study of Bereavement." *Journal of Thanatology* 2(Summer-Fall): 865-866.

Klerman, G. L., and J. E. Izen. 1977. "The Effects of Bereavement and Grief on Physical Health and General Well-Being." *Advances in Psychosomatic Medicine* 9: 63-104.

Kraus, A. S., and A. M. Lilienfeld. 1959. "Some Epidemiological Aspects of the High Mortality Rate in the Young Widowed Group." *Journal of Chronic Disease* 10: 207-217.

Lehrman, S. R. 1956. "Reactions to Untimely Death." *Psychiatric Quarterly* 30: 564-578.

McMahon, B., and T. F. Pugh. 1965. "Suicide in the Widowed." *American Journal of Epidemiology* 81: 23-31.

McNeill, D. N. 1973. "Mortality Among the Widowed in Connecticut." M.P.H. essay, New Haven: Yale University.

Palgi, P. 1973. "The Socio-Cultural Expressions and Implications of Death, Mourning and Bereavement Arising Out of the War in Israel." *Israel Annals of Psychiatry* 2(4): 301-329.

Parkes, C. M., B. Benjamin, and R. G. Fitzgerald. 1969. "Broken Heart: A Statistical Study of Increased Mortality Among Widowers." *British Medical Journal* 1: 740-743.

Parkes, C. M. 1975. "Unexpected and Untimely Bereavement: A Statistical Study of Young Boston Widows and Widowers." In B. Schoenberg, I. Gerber, A. Wiener, A. W. Kutscher, D. Peretz, and A. C. Carr, eds. *Bereavement: Its Psychosocial Aspects*. New York: Columbia University Press.

Paykel, E., J. K. Meyers, M. N. Dienelt, G. L. Klerman, J. J. Lindenthal, and M. P. Pepper. 1969. "Life Events and Depression. A Controlled Study." *Archives of General Psychiatry* 21: 753-760.

Purisman, R., and B. Maoz. 1977. "Adjustment and War Bereavement. Some Considerations." *British Journal of Medical Psychology* 50: 1-9.

Rahe, R. H. 1975. "Epidemiological Studies of Life Change and Illness." *International Journal of Psychiatry in Medicine* 6(1-2): 133-136.

Rees, W. D., and S. G. Lutkins. 1967. "Mortality of Bereavement." *British Medical Journal* 4: 13-16.

Richards, J. G., and J. McCullum. 1979. "Bereavement in the Elderly." *New Zealand Medical Journal* 89(632): 201-204.

Sanders, C. M. 1979-1980. "A Comparison of Adult Bereavement in the Death of Spouse, Child, and Parent." *Omega* 10(4): 303-322.

Schwab, J. J., J. M. Chalmers, S. J. Conroy, P. B. Farris, and R. E. Markush. 1975. "Studies in Grief: A Preliminary Report." In B. Schoenberg, I. Gerber, A. Wiener, A. H. Kutscher, D. Peretz, and A. C. Carr, eds. *Bereavement: Its Psychosocial Aspects*. New York: Columbia University Press.

Ward, A. W. M. 1976. "Mortality of Bereavement." *British Medical Journal* 1: 700-702.

Part II

Grief in Selected
Loss Relationships

11

Bereft and Bereaved: Grief in Nontraditional Relationships

Kenneth J. Doka

> During the last two preconvention counselor training
> sessions, little or no information was provided re-
> garding counseling individuals living alternative life-
> styles. That group has been defined as including all
> those people who are not heterosexual, monogamous,
> white, married, and middle class. (*Newletter of the
> Forum for Death Education and Counseling* 1981)

The authors of this letter do well in focusing on an increasingly evident problem. Despite growing research on grief and
bereavement and the burgeoning interest in this field, little
consideration has been given to the issue of grief in nontraditional relationships. As early as 1976, Folta and Deck noted:

> While all of these studies tell us that grief is a
> normal phenomenon, the intensity of which corre-
> sponds to the closeness of the relationship with the
> deceased, they fail to take this (i.e., friendship)
> into account. The underlying assumption is that
> "closeness of relationship" exists only among spouses
> and/or immediate kin.
>   Even in the case of friendship, the role of friend
> is recognized and the friend may be accorded some
> opportunity, albeit a small one, to publicly acknowl-
> edge and mourn the loss.

Nontraditional relationships are loosely defined as ones that
have limited public acceptance and legal standing, and that
may face some degree of negative sanction within the larger
community. Included here are extramarital affairs, cohabitation,
and homosexual relationships.

It is evident that many such relationships exist. Estimates
have indicated that more than 1 million couples are presently
cohabitating (Reiss 1980) and that an overwhelming majority
of these couples are looking toward eventual marriage (Bower

and Christopherson 1977). There are also very rough estimates that 40 to 50 percent of married men and women have had at least one extramarital affair (Reiss 1980). Again, rough estimates indicate that approximately 3 percent of males and 2 to 3 percent of females are exclusively homosexual and that similar percentages have had mixed homosexual and heterosexual experiences (Gagnon 1977).

Though there has been some research on aging male homosexuals that noted that grief and bereavement are among the problems of aging (Kelly 1977; Kimmel 1978, 1979), and other research has discussed bereavement counseling as part of the supportive services offered to AIDS victims (Heinemann et al. 1983), research on grief in other nontraditional relationships is virtually nonexistent.

This chapter focuses on grief in nontraditional relationships. Using existing literature and six case studies, we consider four related issues. First, we consider the ways in which the resolution of bereavement is complicated in nontraditional relationships. Second, we describe common manifestations of atypical grief that may be evident in nontraditional relationships. Third, we discuss five dimensions that affect the resolution of grief in nontraditional relationships. Finally, we offer suggestions to be used in counseling the survivors of nontraditional relationships.

SPECIFIC PROBLEMS OF GRIEF IN NONTRADITIONAL RELATIONSHIPS

Intense Negative Affect

Myriad emotions are associated with normal grief. The bereaved frequently experience feelings of anger, guilt, sadness and depression, loneliness, hopelessness, and numbness (Worden 1982; Glick, Weiss and Parkes 1974; Lindemann 1944). These emotions are often intensified in nontraditional relationships.

Because these relationships are negatively sanctioned, feelings of guilt may be particularly evident. This guilt may be manifested in two ways. In some cases, the bereaved person may believe that the relationship itself was a factor in the death. For example, in one case a woman was mourning the loss of a man with whom she had had an affair for a number of years. Although the affair had terminated almost a year prior to his death, she still had strong feelings of guilt. She wondered how much the strain of the affair—the secrecy, the excitement, and the added tension at home—had contributed to his fatal attack.

In another case, a 30-year-old woman had terminated a relationship with a married man after he had suffered a mild heart attack because she feared the embarrassment that would

ensue if he suffered a fatal attack at her home. When he died
in an accident some eight months later, she felt guilt that she
had been, as she stated, "so selfish and callous." Heinemann
et al. (1983), in their work with the lovers of AIDS victims,
found that many had a deep sense of guilt over life-style factors that may have contributed to the disease.

In other cases, the general nature of the relationship may
contribute to feelings of guilt. For example, a 40-year-old
woman who had had an affair with a neighbor who was dying
of cancer stated, "I keep thinking that maybe this is a punishment for what I did. Whenever his wife tells me how much he
is suffering, I keep thinking it is because of us. I want to
pray, but I don't ever go to church. . . ." This comment
illustrates another problem that is inherent in nontraditional
relationships, a strong sense of alienation from sources of
solace such as religion.

Other emotions may be intensified. The survivor may exhibit considerable anger over being deserted in such an unten-
able situation. Survivors may experience extreme isolation and
deep loneliness.

Often, these relationships are also highly ambivalent. The
initial response to death may even be a sense of emancipation
or euphoria. As one woman in an extramarital affair stated,
"I was trying to end it for a while. When he died, I thought,
'This is it—this is finally it.' I felt sad, but also relieved."
However, as Worden (1982) has pointed out, such feelings
are often short-lived.

Exclusion of the Dying from Care and Support

Often care of the dying person can facilitate grief adjustment (Homovitch 1964). However, those in nontraditional relationships are frequently excluded from an active role in the
care of the dying. In some cases, the exclusion may be physical. Intensive care units often limit visiting privileges to the
immediate family. Both Kimmel (1978) and Kelly (1977) found
that the male homosexuals in their samples complained that
such restrictions, as well as the attitudes of medical staff,
inhibited anticipatory grief.

In other situations, the constraints of the nontraditional
role can inhibit signs of care or emotional leave-takings. For
the woman who had had an affair with her neighbor, visiting
was limited to making neighborly calls with her husband, or
in some cases, providing support to the wife. "I would look
at him and want to say so much—do something—but couldn't
do more than exchange pleasantries. There was so much I
wanted to say. His wife would thank me profusely for coming,
which even made me feel worse. . . ."

In another case, a secretary who was having an affair
with a man at work could only visit him with the rest of the

workers. "I often used to press his secretary to visit L, so that I could go with her. I had to stand silently by. Whenever I pushed to go more than once a week, his secretary would joke and say, 'I just saw him Tuesday, his wife will think I'm having an affair with him.'"

Lack of Social Support

One factor that is critical in facilitating bereavement is the presence of social support (Parkes 1980). Too often, this is lacking in nontraditional relationships. The grief may have to remain private. One woman who had been involved in an office extramarital affair noted, "I could only share it with my best friend. She was the only one I told about it. A few times I broke up in the office, and when anyone asked what was wrong, I would only say 'nothing.' All sorts of stories floated around the office—I was dying, my kid was on dope. . . ."

Another woman who had been cohabiting with a man for two years described a similar lack of social support when her lover died. "While he was alive, we had good rapport with his family. We visited, exchanged gifts and favors. During the funeral, they occasionally introduced me to distant relatives as a 'friend' or 'girlfriend' of J's. After the funeral I dropped by, but they were very cold. It was clear that my relationship with his parents was finished."

The lack of social support continues after the death. A surviving spouse has the role, however vague, of "widow." The survivor of a nontraditional relationship has no such role. As one woman who was cohabitating said, "I don't even know what I am. How will I explain this to my future husband or kids? He was more than a boyfriend, less than a husband. What am I now?"

Exclusion from Funeral Rituals

Persons in nontraditional relationships may be denied any role in planning or participating in funeral rituals. Sometimes the secrecy of the relationship inhibits any role. As one woman commented:

> When F finally died, I went to the funeral with the girls from the office. Everything was very perfunctory. They planned to get there right before the service, give their condolences, and leave. While the priest was speaking about all the family he had left behind, I kept thinking "What about me?" And all through the sermon, L kept whispering "Come on already, I'm dying for a drink. . . ."

At other times, the exclusion may be unintentional. Often the family "circles its wagons" at the time of a death. Those outside of immediate kinship can easily be forgotten. Folta and Deck (1976) found that friends were frequently not consulted at a death. Kimmel (1978) found a similar complaint among homosexuals. In an illustrative case, a homosexual recounted, "M and I were lovers for years. When M died, his brother called me to tell me the funeral arrangements. I said, 'You didn't consult me?' He replied, in a surprised way, 'The family has a lot on their minds.'"

In other situations the exclusion can be deliberate. In one case of cohabitation, the survivor reported that "the family made it very clear—I could come, but they would choose the [funeral] home, the time, the hymns, everything. We had people at the funeral over after [i.e., the interment]. I brought lasagna. His mother wouldn't put it out. It wouldn't 'go' with the ham and turkey."

In some cases, the exclusion is total. Sometimes, because of the clandestine and sporadic nature of the relationship, the survivor does not even learn of the death until weeks after the event.

In any case, the sanctions against attempting anything but a discreet distance are severe. One letter to Ann Landers notes the severe disapproval extended to those who violate such limits.

> Last week another long-time acquaintance passed away. His secretary wailed and sobbed so loudly during the service, everyone wanted to know who she was. The widow's sister told us later she was her brother-in-law's secretary and sweetheart for several years. The widow wanted to have her thrown out but she didn't wish to make a scene.
>
> What is wrong with these women that they don't have the decency to stay away from the family at such a time?

Legal Difficulties

Finally, there are legal problems. As Kelly (1977) stated, there may be problems of inheritance when an individual dies intestate or when a survivor becomes involved in legal battles with the deceased's relatives; problems of ownership when one party in joint ownership dies; and difficulties that arise from the fact that the survivor has no legal standing and therefore cannot sue in cases of wrongful death.

IMPLICATIONS FOR GRIEF RESOLUTION

These special difficulties combine to complicate grieving in the survivors of nontraditional relationships. Worden (1982) has suggested that the resolution of grief involves four tasks. These are: accepting the reality of loss; experiencing the pain of grief; adjusting to an environment from which the deceased is missing; and withdrawing emotional energy from the deceased and reinvesting it in others.

The problems cited earlier can impair the resolution of these tasks. It is more difficult to accept the reality of a death if one has been excluded from the process leading to it, if one has been cut off from the funeral rituals and restrained from acknowledging the loss, or if one's knowledge of the death has been delayed. The intense, complicated, and ambivalent emotions associated with nontraditional relationships can constrain affective progress. The sensitive, sometimes secretive and even exciting nature of the relationship may make replacement difficult. In addition, traditional sources of solace such as ritual and religion may complicate rather than facilitate grief work. Formal and informal systems of support may not be available or helpful.

Given these circumstances, atypical manifestations of grief are not unusual. Since resolution of the tasks of mourning is impaired, grief can become chronic. In other cases, the secretive nature of the relationship and the lack of social support may lead to delayed or masked grief reactions. Sometimes the latter might emerge in physical illness or unusual behavior. In one case, a woman who had been very careful to maintain discretion in her affair with a married man began, after his death, to engage in openly provocative and flirtatious actions in her office. Bowlby (1980) has suggested that sometimes the bereaved may become so euphoric that their mood can be described as a manic episode. Although I have not observed such reactions, and Bowlby (1980) did not find them to be common, it is logical to expect them to occur in nontraditional relationships.

DIMENSIONS OF NONTRADITIONAL RELATIONSHIPS

In addition to the aspects of grief commonly found in nontraditional relationships, it also is evident that the nature of these relationships can vary in a number of ways.

Some of these relationships may be very open, whereas others are quite secret. Thus, the relationship can be known only to the involved parties, can be shared with their intimates, or can be generally known. The more open the relationship, the more opportunities there will be to acknowledge grief and receive social support.

Another critical dimension is the degree to which a person has invested in a relationship. As Reiss (1980) discussed, extramarital relationships may range from casual flings to more serious and sustained commitments. This leads to another dimension: the meaning that the relationship has for the parties involved. Each relationship supports some sense of self. It is essential to consider what aspects of self are supported by a relationship and how that support will be maintained in the absence of the relationship. Some of the attributes may be very positive. The relationship may support attributes of desirability or importance. However, there may be negative effects as well.

The opportunity to find replacements for the lost relationship is another variable in nontraditional relationships. In some cases there may be many opportunities to reinvest in other relationships; in other cases, the opportunities may be limited and be accompanied by risks. Finally, there is the dimension of acceptance or rejection; that is, the degree to which the relationship is accepted or rejected by significant others.

Nontraditional relationships may be viewed as part of a series of continuums. At one pole might be relationships that are open, accepted, and involve high degrees of commitment and affect, but that will provide opportunities for replacement. In contemporary American society, heterosexual cohabitation would fall close to this pole. In these cases, grief may approximate that of spouses, albeit without some of the traditional sources of support. Homosexual and extramarital relationships may be at the other pole of this continuum. In these relationships, myriad combinations may complicate grief considerably.

SUGGESTIONS FOR COUNSELING

It is beyond the scope of this chapter to provide an extensive discussion of the nature of grief counseling and therapy. However, a few comments may be cogent. I begin with Worden's (1982) contention that the goal of grief counseling is to facilitate the client's resolution of the tasks of grief. Thus, in nontraditional relationships, it may first be necessary to define the nature of the relationship and to assess the ways in which the resolution of grief has been impaired. As noted earlier, in some cases the grief may be masked. It is not unusual to see the client initially focus on another issue.

The counselor has to be extremely sensitive to the moral ambiguity that may surround such relationships. Clients may be highly defensive. In some cases, they may actively seek the counselor's approval of the relationship. In others, they may seek condemnation. This defensive and ambivalent context suggests caution.

As part of grief resolution, it is important to find meaning and purpose in the relationship. I try to have clients affirm, within their own beliefs and ethics, the value of the association. When it is appropriate and needed, and again within their own religious and ethical convictions, clients may accept and extend forgiveness.

Since these relationships are often ambiguous and, in the aftermath of death, unfinished, there are a few techniques that I have found especially helpful. A letter to the deceased or a discussion with an empty chair can often provide needed closure. Assisting the client in developing alternative rituals can also facilitate resolution.

CONCLUSION

It should be recognized that many of the variables that generally affect the intensity of grief, such as the circumstances of the death, the nature of the relationship, or the characteristics of the bereaved, affect grief in nontraditional relationships as well. Grief in nontraditional relationships is but one aspect of grief. It is that truism that counselors, educators, and researchers in the field need to recognize.

REFERENCES

Bower, D., and V. Christopherson. 1977. "University Student Cohabitation: A Regional Comparison of Selected Attitudes and Behavior." *Journal of Marriage and the Family* 39: 447-453.

Bowlby, J. 1980. *Attachment and Loss*, Vol. 3. New York: Basic Books.

Folta, J., and E. Deck. 1976. "Grief, the Funeral and the Friends." In V. Pine et al., eds. *Acute Grief and the Funeral*, pp. 231-240. Springfield, IL: Charles C. Thomas.

Gagnon, J. H. 1977. *Human Sexualities*. Glenview, IL: Scott, Foreman & Co.

Glick, I., R. Weiss, and C. M. Parkes. 1974. *The First Years of Bereavement*. New York: Wiley.

Heinemann, A., G. Soucy, D. Richards, and H. McMillan. 1983. "A Social Service Program for AIDS Clients." Presented at the Annual Meeting of the Forum for Death Education and Counseling, Chicago, IL, Oct. 21.

Homovitch, M. 1964. "The Aging Male Homosexual: Myth and Reality." *Gerontologist* 17: 328-332.

Kimmel, D. 1978. "Adult Development and Aging: A Gay Perspective." *Journal of Social Issues* 34:113-131.

Kimmel, D. 1979. "Life-History Interviews of Aging Gay Men." *International Journal of Aging and Human Development* 10: 239-248.

Lindemann, E. 1944. "Symptomatology and the Management of Acute Grief." *American Journal of Psychiatry* 101: 131-149.

Newletter of the Forum for Death Education and Counseling. 1981. 5: 2.

Parkes, C. M. 1980. "Bereavement Counseling: Does It Work?" *British Medical Journal* 281: 3-6.

Reiss, I. 1980. *Family Systems in America* (3rd ed.). New York: Holt, Rinehart and Winston.

Worden, W. 1982. *Grief Counseling and Grief Therapy.* New York: Springer.

12

In-Laws as Mutual Helpers
in Grief

Joseph A. Healy

Wherever you go, I will go,
   Wherever you live, I will live.
Your people shall be my people,
   and your God, my God.
Wherever you die, I will die
   and there I will be buried.
May Yahweh do this thing to me
   and more also,
   if even death should come between us.

        —Book of Ruth 1:16-17

Most of us recognize these words, having heard them at many
weddings. The sentiments seem appropriate to a couple launch-
ing their adult lives together in marriage. I wonder, though,
how many realize that these words from the biblical story of
Ruth were spoken by neither bride nor groom, nor were they
addressed to a beloved spouse. Rather, they came from the
heart and mouth of a young woman, recently widowed, and
expressed a commitment to a similarly bereaved but unlikely
beloved, her mother-in-law. Such devotion contrasts sharply,
to say the least, with the stereotype of that kind of relationship. Yet Naomi, who was grieving for a husband and two
sons, with Ruth and Orpah, her widowed daughters-in-law,
formed the first recorded bereavement support group. Ruth's
declaration provides an apt introduction to discussion on the
grief of a parent for an adult child.

I am the executive director of THEOS, an international
mutual self-help network of young and middle-aged widowed
men and women. For this brief study, I interviewed three
men and two women, and wish to share their reflections on
the "in-law connection" of the grief process. The sampling is
not scientific, their experience is not universal, and their
recommendations are not absolute. Nevertheless, they deserve
a hearing because they strongly suggest that the quality of

the in-law relationship during marriage can have a significant impact—for better or for worse—on recovery from the death of the one who linked them.

WARREN

Now in his late 20's and widowed two years ago, Warren shared four years of marriage. He and his wife had no children. He reports that although they lived in different states, his wife and her family enjoyed a relationship expressed through three or four phone calls a month to her parents and monthly correspondence with her sister. His own relationship with his in-laws developed, but slowly.

His wife's one-and-a-half year illness brought Warren and his in-laws closer. Seven or eight phone calls and at least one visit a month marked their communication. He and his in-laws provided support for each other in the immediate aftermath of her death, cooperatively planning the funeral and carrying out the services. Some tension over the disposition of his wife's possessions constituted the only significantly negative element in their interaction.

In regard to dealing with their grief, Warren notes the following differences. His parents-in-law seemed more "relieved" than he over the end of his wife's suffering. They appeared, to him, to accept and recover from her death sooner and better than he, emphasizing the past through gratitude for her life. He describes himself, on the other hand, as having been initially bitter because of the future destroyed by her death.

However, Warren's long-term adjustment sounds better balanced than that of the parents. His mother-in-law visits her daughter's grave almost weekly, and her church and community work sometimes appears as "busy-ness," activity for the sake of distraction. The father-in-law has taken the approach of significant social withdrawal, masking his feelings behind what his son-in-law calls "Swedish stoicism." But Warren portrays himself now, after two years, in these words: "I feel better than ever . . . not as happy as I was . . . but able to enjoy life again. . . ." He acknowledges that he misses his wife and cherishes mementoes of her, but he socializes quite a bit and has a life-style he enjoys. He identifies involvement in a mutual self-help group and a return to school as key factors in his recovery.

The relationship between Warren and his parents-in-law has deepened since the death of their loved one. They communicated by phone and mail monthly during the first year and have done so every other month since then. Warren concludes by saying that "We are still growing closer to each other."

SALLY

Sally, now in her early 50's and with three grown children, considers it significant that her husband was an only child and that his parents were elderly when he was diagnosed as a victim of cancer. His parents had become very dependent on her husband, and Sally perceived herself as a "buffer" between him and his parents. Prior to her husband's illness, the couple communicated with his parents by weekly phone calls and two or three visits annually.

Sally's husband's extended illness and treatments limited those visits to one or two a year, but the weekly phone calls continued. However, from Sally's viewpoint, her father-in-law's tendency to "dump" on his son added to the stress of his illness. What worsened the relationship was the fact that her father-in-law ignored his son's terminal illness and never even acknowledged Sally's letter detailing the diagnosis and prognosis. As it turned out, Sally's father-in-law died a year before his son did, and her mother-in-law's mental state made it futile even to inform her of her son's death.

CHARLES

Charles and his wife of 35 years lived in the same area as his in-laws and they experienced a very close relationship, before, during, and after Charles' marriage. Charles reports that

the relationship between his wife and her mother deepened after their marriage;

his in-laws regularly served as baby sitters;

the two families took extended trips together;

his father-in-law was an "outstanding person."

Charles's wife's illness lasted two-and-a-half years, and he cites "relief" as the dominant reaction to her death. Her mother, in the meantime, had also fallen ill and died within days of her daughter, which compounded the grief of their survivors. Charles's father-in-law considered himself to have healing power in his hands and, to a certain extent, felt that the deaths of his daughter and his wife were failures on his part. He moved to the West Coast, went into a deep depression, and died within a few years. The illness and death of three very significant people within five years made it extremely difficult for Charles to take a positive approach to the future. He took early retirement from his job, but now has begun to reestablish a social life. He credits his sister-in-law as a major influence in "getting me out of the house and involved in things." About his father-in-law, Charles says that, regarding the quality of Charles's relationship with his own daughter-in-law and grandchild, "some of him rubbed off on me."

JERRY

Jerry had been married and divorced, but was childless when he married a woman who had spent some years in a convent. Their only child, a daughter, was five years old when Jerry's wife died. After her death, which occurred five years ago, Jerry married again, but has since been separated.

In outlining his relationship with his in-laws prior to his wife's illness and death, Jerry cited the following factors as significant:

his previous divorce and his wife's departure from the convent caused her parents to disapprove of their marriage;

his father-in-law's death increased the mother-in-law's dependence on her daughter;

the birth of their daughter helped to bridge gaps between Jerry and his wife and her parents.

The two families lived 150 miles apart, but exchanged phone calls every few weeks and six to eight visits annually.

Jerry didn't offer specific comparisons between his own and his mother-in-law's coping styles, but he made comments about their relationship. During his marriage, Jerry felt gradually more accepted as a person by his in-laws. His daughter's birth and his wife's illness deepened that relationship. Moreover, her own widowhood intensified his mother-in-law's appreciation of family relationships. The depth of this relationship was partially manifested in the openness with which his mother-in-law accepted Jerry's subsequent and brief marriage. Her positive attitude included inviting the new "family" to visit in her home.

Jerry emphasized the value of the relationship for his daughter and her grandmother. For an only child, in-laws can constitute the only "family" the child has. His daughter has an annual monthlong visit with her grandmother, during which they share memories and mementos of the daughter-mother they each loved and lost. Moreover, Jerry has found a supportive friend in his brother-in-law, whose child is the equivalent of a sibling for his daughter.

As a kind of postscript, Jerry noted that his own mother died when he was about the same age that his daughter was when her mother died. Thus, his daughter knew from his example that one could survive such an experience and lead a fulfilling life.

MARY

Mary and her husband were in their early 40's and had five sons when he died after a brief illness. Her mother-in-law had fit the stereotype of dependent wife until she was widowed at a young age. At that time she transferred her dependency to her son, then 16. Even after her son's marriage to Mary, he continued to be his mother's chief resource. They lived in the same town, had weekly communication, and spent holidays together.

The imbalance in the relationship tended to make Mary and her in-laws competitors rather than companions in grief, as illustrated by the following.

The mother explicitly claimed that the death of a son is worse than the death of a husband.

The obituary accidentally but significantly described the deceased first as "son of," then as "husband of" and "father of."

The mother also seemed to Mary to have amnesia about her own widowhood and provided no moral support, having, in Mary's words "a one-way phone: it takes only incoming calls."

Mary's brothers-in-law acted similarly in that their brother's death seemed to end their relationship with Mary and her sons; they initiated no phone calls or visits.

At a nephew's graduation party, both brothers visited on the porch, but did not enter the house.

Five years after the death, a nephew's wedding reception marked the first time one brother talked to Mary about her husband and her children.

Mary acknowledges that this behavior caused her to feel great anger and resentment, especially since her five sons lacked the kind of male role models that more sensitive uncles could have provided. However, she takes pride in the fact that she did not give up on her in-laws and that her initiative has recently resulted in improved relationships. She provided her own home as a convalescent place for her mother-in-law for several months and she has fostered mutual visits with siblings-in-law. In this way, she has lived up to her own values and maintained her sons' links to their paternal roots.

RECOMMENDATIONS

I asked the five people who participated in this survey to make suggestions about how bereaved individuals and their in-laws might more effectively help each other. The following composite of their comments is addressed primarily to married people, but should be useful to professional caregivers in their counseling role. Some of these suggestions have the sound of cliches. However, I read somewhere that the only way to make cliches come alive is to take them seriously.

1. Married people would do well, ideally before crises occur,
   a. to evaluate and rank the personal pros and cons of maintaining or strengthening their relationships with each other's families, e.g., as a link to a shared loved one or as extended family for their children;
   b. to do whatever it takes to work at these relationships in accord with their evaluation, for example by maintaining their availability to their in-laws, by providing quality time together, by taking initiative and even sometimes by swallowing their pride and giving others the benefit of doubts;
   c. to give and take suggestions precisely as such— that is, as suggestions, not as interference.

2. Parents should also be mindful of the likelihood that their children will follow patterns they set. The traditions they establish as sons- and daughters-in-law might determine their experience as parents-in-law.

3. During the initial stages of grief, the widowed and their in-laws might aid each other's healing if they
   a. spend time together;
   b. allow each other distinctive forms of expressing grief;
   c. provide each other with reassurances that "we are still family" and that their relationship will survive.

4. In the long term, my interviewees urged that
   a. channels of communication be kept open through mail, phone calls, and, especially, visits;
   b. each person seek to understand the other's experience and viewpoint;
   c. each person seek to foster a positive attitude that "good times are still possible";
   d. parents-in-law be open and supportive about remarriage;
   e. widowed people who remarry assure grandparents of continuing "visitation" arrangements;
   f. relationships among cousins be fostered, especially for "only children" whose parents have died.

For professionals who serve married and widowed people, my consultants suggested the following:

1. In whatever way you can, promote consideration of the above recommendations for bereaved families.

2. Encourage bereaved families to acknowledge their in-laws and to involve them appropriately in consultations about such things as prognosis, funeral services, future plans.

3. Be alert to the varied, specific, and long-term needs of bereaved families and, according to your specialized role, remain available as a direct resource and/or referral agent.

4. Beyond your work with specific individuals and families, explicitly seek recognition of in-laws as an integral part of the immediate or extended family, e.g., by finding ways to instill attitudes that recognize that in-law relationships can create bonds beyond the legal and beyond dependence on the shared person.

CONCLUSION

In the biblical story with which I began, Naomi "rewarded" Ruth's loyalty by moving from mother-in-law to matchmaker and helping Ruth to find a new husband. Even if such a pay-back were guaranteed, perhaps no contemporary widow or widower would offer to give up God and country out of loyalty to a mother-in-law. Nevertheless, the friends whose stories and suggestions I have shared would agree: marriages that last "until death" need not break the ties or destroy the bonds they created among those whom a dead person loved—deeply but differently—as son or daughter or spouse.

13

The Forgotten Men: Concern for Widowers

Edie J. Smith

Across the United States, community-based services to the widowed, most of which are provided through self-help groups, continue to reach thousands of newly widowed people. With the support of others in their circumstances, the newly widowed are working toward the meaningful resolution of their grief. Each year, for every three women who experience the loss of a spouse, there are two men who experience the same devastating loss. However, the participation of widowers in the Widowed Persons Service (WPS) and other bereavement self-help groups is less than one man to ten women.

Recent research has caused increased concern about this disproportionate participation. Studies indicate that for at least the first four months after the death of his wife, a man's health is in extreme jeopardy. As a result of stress, his immunological level is so low that he is very vulnerable to emotional or physical illness (Schleifer et al. 1983).

Statistics paint a grim picture of the stress of surviving one's wife. Widowers die four times as often from suicide, three times as often from automobile accidents, ten times as often from strokes, and six times as often from heart disease as do married men of the same ages. This high death rate among widowed men justifies concern (Helsong and Szklo 1981). The high divorce rate among the 52 percent of widowers who remarry within the first 18 months after the death of a wife is another concern. It is estimated that over half of these early remarriages end in divorce or abandonment (*U.S. News and World Report* 1981).

Our goal is to make WPS programming more responsive to widowers.

WIDOWERS' TASK FORCE

In 1983, the WPS gave top priority to meeting the needs of widowers by asking them what they felt, what they needed,

and how we could effectively meet those needs. A Widowers'
Task Force of eight men was established. Six of the men had
been widowed. All of them were involved in local WPS programming. Stephen Alexander, Patrick Briese, John Downing,
Robert Farra, Robert Gray, Ray Gould, Les Monson, and
Robert Utzinger met to talk about the myths or assumptions
they and we have to overcome in order to provide support to
grieving men, as well as the feelings and needs of these men
and their fears about looking for help and support. After
this, they discussed and worked on plans for action that our
local programs can use to ease widowers' pain. Jane Johnston,
leadership development specialist, and I, both staff members of
the American Association of Retired Persons (AARP), developed
the format for the meetings, guided some of the discussions,
and recorded all relevant material.

The following is a summary of the Widowers' Task Force
discussions.

MAJOR PROBLEMS OR NEEDS OF
NEWLY WIDOWED MEN

The Task Force and other research identified some of the
major problems and needs that widowers face:

- Lack of someone with whom they can share the intimacy
  they shared with their wives. Widowers say that loneliness
  is their most serious problem. For many men, loneliness
  is intensified by the fact that they have had no serious
  friendships with either men or women other than their
  wives.

- Inability to keep house and maintain home life the way it
  was maintained when the wife was alive. Men wish to be
  self-sufficient, but the tasks they have to learn, such as
  cooking, cleaning, and other self-maintenance chores,
  seem overwhelming at first.

- Lack of contact with other widowed men. Most widowers
  cannot readily find other widowers with whom to communicate.

- Little preparation for what had been largely "maternal
  functions," such as child care. This is a particular problem for younger widowers. The triple burden of caring for
  children, household, and self can be crippling when a man
  doesn't have the necessary skills prior to his wife's death.
  Older and younger widowers have problems communicating
  effectively with their children in both practical and emotional matters.

- Loss of social connections, especially those that are couple-
  oriented. Widowhood is often most difficult for older widow-

ers who have retired. In addition to widowhood, they may be adjusting to the loss of job-role status and the loss of social relations developed on the job.

BARRIERS TO HELP

The Task Force identified two major barriers to helping widowers. The first barrier consists of assumptions held by both men and women. Here are a few:

ASSUMPTION: "Widowers have an easier time of it than widows." We often hear that men have meaningful work to throw themselves into, that they easily find new social contacts, that couples are delighted to include an extra man in their activities, and that matchmakers abound for widowers.

REALITY: Men often do throw themselves into work. However, their confusion and pain usually make this work less meaningful to them. They rarely find new social contacts, and most often spend their time at home with no one to talk to. They feel strange and alienated when couples ask them out, and they are afraid of meeting or dating new women at this vulnerable time in their lives. Widowers' feelings, in short, are very similar to those of widows.

ASSUMPTION: "Men don't grieve as long or as much as women."

REALITY: Men have intense feelings of sadness, loneliness, helplessness, indecision, guilt, anger, and depression. Because men in our society feel uncomfortable expressing these feelings openly, the assumption is made by both men and women that men do not have these feelings. Many men cannot label their feelings. However, it is safe to say that because men's feelings are unexpressed or repressed, they are more intense and last longer. As a result, men may also experience physical ailments. Men's timetables for grieving vary as much from individual to individual as women's do.

ASSUMPTION: "Men just want a housekeeper to do their cooking and cleaning. They just 'replace' the deceased spouse to get someone to take care of them."

REALITY: Men experience great difficulty in learning the new skills they need. But, more often than not, they are willing to learn these skills. At first, tasks they haven't had to do before seem overwhelming and they find it hard to cope. The man who can change a tire with ease may not know how to begin to fill a dishwasher or peel a vegetable.

ASSUMPTION: "Men are just looking for sex and they can usually find it."

REALITY: Most men experience a lack of interest in sex during the grieving process. However, their need for intimacy is very strong. Many widowers (and the widows who have tried to help them) confuse this desperate need for someone to comfort them, listen to them, and understand them with a desire for sex.

ASSUMPTION: "Men prefer to talk to women about their feelings; they don't want to share their intimate problems with another man."
REALITY: Many men do prefer to share their feelings with women. Many others do because they don't feel that they have the option of talking to a man. However, many men are afraid to talk to women during the grieving process. They feel that women will ask them to be strong and will want them, in turn, to listen to them talk about their problems. They cannot carry another's burdens at this time. Also, many men feel guilty at sharing their intimate lives with another woman so soon after the death of their wives. Given the option, men would often choose to talk to another man because they would prefer to talk for a while about other subjects than their feelings before reaching into their pain.

The core assumption in all of this is that a man's feelings following the death of a mate are somehow different, in degree or kind, from those of a woman. We have found that there are differences in the degree of intensity, but very little difference in the feelings themselves. What is different is the way widowers view themselves. Widowers' behaviors often mask their inner feelings. Our approaches to helping widowers within WPS can be more effective if we understand this.

The second barrier to be overcome in providing help to a widower is his fear, primarily his fear of looking for or accepting help. Society, together with most of our families, has provided us with a myth about men: *Men must be strong and self-sufficient.* This myth, which has been made a reality that is shared by men and women alike, is at the heart of many widowers' fear of seeking help or support.

Another type of shock that men have expressed after losing their wives is the realization, perhaps for the first time in their lives, that *they are not as strong and self-sufficient as they had believed.* As one of the members of our Task Force put it, "To take that first step to accept help was to admit to myself and the world that I was not." For men, not to be strong or self-sufficient is to be unmanly in their own eyes. Not to be "macho," in common jargon, is, unfortunately, to be considered a "wimp." Widowers' other fears include:

1. The *fear of disclosing weakness, vulnerability, and "unacceptable" feelings before they are ready.* "I may break

down. I may cry. I may make a fool of myself in front of everybody."

2. The *fear of rejection*. "If I were to attend a group or meeting, maybe they wouldn't accept me. Maybe my problems are different. Maybe nobody will talk to me."

3. The *fear of being outnumbered by women*. "When I was growing up, I knew widows who were friends of our family, but I never knew a widower. I may be the only man in this town who is going through this."

4. The *fear of being pressured to be a leader*. "Groups expect men to take over leadership roles, especially groups that are predominantly attended by women. I can barely do my job now; I can't take on more work."

5. The *fear of the unknown*. "I wanted to know in great detail who sponsored this program, what it was about, what they did and why."

These fears are formidable barriers to overcome. However, the men on our Task Force were willing to share them with us and each other. They *did* get involved with WPS. All are grateful to WPS for the concern and support they received. They are now willing to give to others.

The Task Force members unanimously agree that we cannot easily change the myths by which men and women live. We need to acknowledge that men's fears are potent and strongly ingrained. The Task Force Action Plans for WPS emphasized the idea that we must meet men where they are, not where we or they wish they were.

ACTION PLANS FOR WPS

Each Widowers' Task Force member has submitted an outline of an action plan. Each plan will be implemented to help widowers by offering WPS as a program that is interested in the welfare of widowers as well as widows. The first plan will be to set up male-oriented gatherings. Other plans will deal with setting up a skills exchange between widows and widowers, defining new roles for men in WPS, organizing a speakers bureau for a predominantly male audience, and broadening male representation on WPS boards.

REFERENCES

Helsong, K. J., and M. Szklo. 1981. "Mortality After Bereavement." *American Journal of Epidemiology* (Johns Hopkins University) 114: 1.

"Now Help Is on the Way for Neglected Widowers." 1981. *U.S. News and World Report* (June 22).

Schleifer, S., S. Keller, M. Camerino, J. Thornton, and M. Stein. 1983. "Suppression of Lymphocyte Stimulation Following Bereavement." *Journal of the American Medical Association* 250: 374-377.

14

Children's Reactions to Deaths of Grandparents and Great-Grandparents: Case Histories

Mary-Ellen Siegel

For quite some time, my interest in children's reactions to a grandparent's death has been even more specific than that somewhat broad topic. I wondered just what would be the "right" way to tell a child about a grandparent who died before the child was born.

I remembered learning, as a child, about my grandparents who had died before I was born. Somehow I had always pictured them as shadowy people who had died of old age. Only much later, when I was at the cemetery where they are buried, did I realize that they had not been old. Indeed, my mother had been a teenager when she lost her father, and only a young mother when she lost her mother. My father's mother died when he was only twelve. As is most common, these people were never "introduced" to me during my childhood.

Three and a half years ago, I married a man who was widowed before he became a grandfather. At the time that we announced our plans to marry, he had two grandsons, cousins who were then not quite two. They called him Grandpa, and the question arose: What should they call me? My soon-to-be-stepdaughter asked me what I would like her little boy to call me. "Would 'Grandma' be right?" she asked. I took a deep breath as all my various "hats" jumped on and off. With the stepmother hat on, I thought, "Oh, boy, if I say yes, she may regret it later and be annoyed at me for allowing it. If I say casually, 'Oh, just call me Mary-Ellen,' she may feel rejected, and worse yet, think I am rejecting her child." With my mother hat on, I felt that my own children, particularly my married daughter, might feel slighted if some other child called me Grandma before she had a child.

In the midst of this "catch-22" situation, my social work hat popped onto my head. That's the one that makes me be thoughtful, listen to people, and remain objective, sensitive, sensible, and unselfish. That hat is usually not around when I need it, but that time it was. So I took another deep breath and said, "I think that would only confuse him. Someday when

109

he's a little older he will understand that your mother died
before he was born, and that Grandpa is his grandfather and
I am Grandpa's wife. We can be very special to each other
and he will know that I love him, but that there was a lady
who would be his real grandmother if she had lived. And he
can know about her."

That is how the conversation was left, and the next time
I saw her little boy, he called me Mary-Ellen. By now I have
a very special and warm relationship with him and his cousin,
both of whom are now six. Both of them also understand that
once there was a special lady who would have been their
grandmother, and that many people loved her. Each boy now
has a small brother who also calls me by my first name.

It is difficult to determine how much children at various
stages of development really understand death, especially a
death that took place before they were born. My step-grand-
children see pictures of their parents' wedding. In the pictures, their parents look much as they do today and Grandpa
looks like he does today, but they also see a woman who no
longer is. And of course, I'm not in the pictures.

Children under five, for whom death is often denied as a
final process, may find it easier to understand the finality of
a death that occurred a long time ago than to accept or understand a current death. Young children equate death with separation. They have long since learned that parents go out,
even go on vacations, and then reappear, so that the finality
of death is difficult for them to comprehend.

But in our family there is a grandmother who has never
appeared. There is, however, a nice lady who sits on the floor
and plays with blocks with the children, reads stories, and
makes peanut butter and jelly sandwiches and cupcakes just
for them. In most ways, I am a "grandma." For these children,
perhaps, the idea of permanent loss may be confusing. I have
replaced the grandmother they never had, and this can both
introduce and reinforce children's notion that people can be
replaced, if not actually resurrected. Those of us who have
loved someone who has died know we will never really replace
that person. But we can love someone else who will add joy
and meaning to our lives without becoming a replacement.

But what about a grandparent or great-grandparent who
died before a child was born or when the child was too young
to have any cognitive memory of the person? How can we
"introduce" deceased grandparents to small children without
confusing them or reinforcing unhealthy concepts of death? Or
should we, as my parents did, refrain from any meaningful
descriptions or discussions of the grandparents I never knew?

My mother, who died in 1978, was an important figure in
the lives of all of us. Her young adult grandchildren speak
of her often and have pictures of her in their homes. My own
grandson, who is now three, has recognized her photographs
from the time he could identify pictures, and calls her "Moma."

He now understands that she was my mother and his mother's grandmother. One day when I took him out for pizza I told him that I used to take his mother to the same pizza restaurant and that sometimes his mother's grandmother, "Moma," had taken her there too. Like most children, he likes to hear stories about his parents when they were his age, and we have all agreed that a nice way to introduce him to his "recent roots" is by relating anecdotes that include various great-grandparents. It is our hope that those people who were so important in our lives will come to life for him and that he will not think of them as "shadowy old people" in the past, which was the way I used to perceive my grandparents.

Technology is different today, of course, and so we have many candid photographs of my parents, as well as the formal pictures of our forebears. We also have movies that date back more than fifty years, and we recently put them on videotape. Now we have a convenient, permanent way to introduce those family members who are no longer alive.

A word of caution: introducing deceased family members to young children should be done with care. A youngster who knows that his mother's grandmother is dead might ask *his* grandmother when she will die. It is important that this question be answered with sensitivity and reassurance, but still convey some explanation of the cycle of life and death.

A little over a year ago, my 86-year-old father died. My 22-month-old grandson, Matthew, kept asking, "Papa come car?" They had had a special routine. Papa, as my daughter and Matthew called him, would stop by every few days on his way to work, and they would meet him downstairs in front of their apartment house. Sometimes Papa would let Matthew sit in the car and pretend to drive. The two of them had some wonderful times together.

How do you explain to a not-quite-two-year-old about death? They told him that Papa couldn't come, that he was sick—which he had been—and that he was very old and couldn't get better. Matthew seemed to accept this, but still he continued to ask, "Papa come car?" Then one day he looked at a photograph of Papa and said, "Papa bye-bye," and put his head on his mother's shoulder. His language continued to develop, and one day he looked at a picture of Papa and said, "Matthew miss Papa."

A book I had written with my father was published last May, and there is a photograph of the two of us on the book jacket. Matthew looked at it and said, "Papa and Grandma in that picture." It was clear that Matthew remembered either Papa or Papa's picture. We weren't quite sure which. But then one day I had the promotional material for the book with me when I was at his house. The material contained the same picture that is on the book jacket. Matthew looked at it, looked up at me, then picked up the paper, crumpled it and ran to the wastebasket with it. So you see, even a two-year-old can feel alternately puzzled, sad, angry, and abandoned.

At two-and-a-half, Matthew didn't like to look at pictures of Papa. He would get very sad and close the album. One day in the early fall, he said to his mother, "I don't like to look at the albums." She asked him if it was because the pictures of Papa made him sad. He nodded, and she said, "Let's put them in a special envelope and write 'Papa' on it. Then someday, if you want to, we can look at them."

On Thanksgiving Day, Sesame Street showed a segment about the death of an important character, Mr. Hooper. Mr. Hooper, a regular on the show, ran the Sesame Street grocery store, and Big Bird, who is often described by the producers as "the show's resident five-year-old," loved Mr. Hooper's stories and the birdseed milkshakes he made. The actor who portrayed Mr. Hooper died last year and the show's producers had to decide whether to write Mr. Hooper out of the show, soap-opera style, or to deal with his death honestly. They chose to deal with it honestly, and on the Thanksgiving show Big Bird approached some of the other characters (not the Muppets, but the "grown-up" real people) with several pictures he had drawn of them. They enthusiastically admired the pictures, and then Big Bird showed them his picture of Mr. Hooper. They complimented Big Bird on the excellent likeness, and then Big Bird looked around for Mr. Hooper. One of the actors reminded Big Bird that they had already told him that Mr. Hooper had died. Big Bird then said he would give Mr. Hooper the picture when he returned. The other characters explained the irreversibility of death to Big Bird, who had great difficulty believing that Mr. Hooper would never return, just as he had earlier "not remembered." He also searched for a reason—and was told, "just because." When Big Bird realized that Mr. Hooper would never return, he turned to the concerns with which everyone, children and adults, grapple: *What about me?* Big Bird was reassured to learn that the others would tell him stories and that someone else would be taking over the store and making him his milkshakes. Big Bird wisely said, "It won't be the same." They agreed, but the segment ended with Big Bird and the audience knowing that they would always remember Mr. Hooper, that the picture of him would help them hold onto the memory of him, and that their lives would continue.

My grandson Matthew saw the show three times. At two-and-three-quarters, he was developing more language and concepts. He turned to his mother and said, "Now I know two people who are dead." A little while later he asked where the pictures of Papa were, and she reminded him where they had placed them. He said, "Now we can put them back in the album." And they did.

Like many small children, Matthew loves to look in my pocketbook and see the pictures I carry in my wallet. Recently he asked me why I carry a picture of Papa. I said, "I like to carry the picture because it helps me remember all the good times we had with Papa. Even though we can't see him anymore, we can look at his pictures and remember him, just like Big Bird did with the picture of Mr. Hooper." This was the first time Matthew looked at the pictures of Papa without pushing them aside. I think that it is interesting to note that sometimes television or media can introduce or reinforce important and meaningful concepts to a child.

Last June, my stepson's father-in-law died. He had sustained a massive heart attack nine years ago, and since then the family had felt that he was living on "borrowed time." He died in his sleep early one Friday morning. His five-year-old grandson, Eli, had left for school without knowing that his parents were on their way to the house where his beloved grandfather had just died.

My husband and I were at the child's home when he returned from school later that afternoon. He seemed to understand that his grandfather, Sabah (the Hebrew name for grandfather), had died. He didn't seem to show any particular reaction and began to play as usual. His mother had been very worried about his reaction—she herself was mourning deeply, and she asked me how I thought she could handle the entire situation. I reminded her that her son might not yet be able to see death as a final event, and might feel that his grandfather could still see, hear, and feel. I cautioned her against making remarks like "Sabah would have been so proud of you" because, although such remarks can be comforting to an older child or to an adult, a small child may interpret them to mean, "He knows what you are doing." And, of course, if Grandpa knows when you are good, then he also knows when you are bad! I reminded her that a five year old may experience many responses, including somatic complaints, denial, anger at the grandfather who left him, and anger at others who "allowed" this to happen. Her son might also suddenly idealize his grandfather who, although he sometimes did scold, might now be remembered as the person who never found fault, who would have condoned any and or all behavior that would be frowned on by his parents and by his other grandfather. Anxiety and even panic could occur at times, as well as guilt. What five year old hasn't sometimes been too noisy for a grandfather, or hasn't been told, "Sabah can't push you so high on the swings," and so on.

I brought Eli the wonderful book entitled *My Grandpa Died Today* (Fassler 1971). It was a good story for Eli because the story Grandpa seemed a little like his. He interrupted me halfway through it, saying "That's like my Sabah," and began to talk of his beloved grandfather, who had read to him from the Torah and explained so much. Eli immediately asked his father who would now do certain rituals that his grandfather had done, for Eli's parents, like his maternal grandparents, are

Orthodox Jews. Eli knows my husband and I are not Orthodox, and thus did not seem to think that his other grandfather would replace his Sabah in such matters, but needed quick reassurance that his father would do so. He then began to ask how his grandfather had died, and had great difficulty understanding that it was a sudden heart attack, and that there hadn't been time to get him to the hospital. Eli seemed convinced that a hospital, the right doctor, the right medicine—something or someone—should have saved his grandfather. We explained to him that his grandfather was not strong, and indeed had been sick for a while.

Then Eli wanted some assurances that his grandfather had been very old. "How old?" he asked. There was no denying that Grandpa was only sixty-eight. Eli wanted to know everyone's age and began to inquire about everyone's health. He then asked about his father's mother, the grandmother who died before he was born. He wanted to know how old she was and what had happened to her. This evoked fresh grief in his father, for whom the death of his father-in-law was also a profound loss.

We continued the story *My Grandpa Died Today*, and although it made clear the finality of death, it showed that Grandpa wasn't afraid to die and that the boy should not be afraid to live. The reader feels that the memory of the grandfather will stay alive. This wasn't enough for Eli. He wanted us to change the story, to make the grandfather only sick and then get better. His mother said, "No, this is how the story is." Then Eli suggested that maybe the grandfather could come alive again. His mother, not wanting to reinforce the fantasy, said "No, Eli, he can't come alive again." Eli, wiser than we thought, said, "I know my Sabah can't come alive again, but just in the story, please."

A colleague has suggested to me that perhaps Eli was saying that the book was too accepting of the grandfather's death. Eli might have preferred a book that said death was unfair and cruel, for surely that is how everyone in his family felt at that time.

Eli went back and forth believing and not quite believing. He wanted to have a part of Sabah close to him, and asked for his prayer book to have in their home. Then, when he realized that he couldn't read it yet, asked his father to read it, but he wanted to keep it in his own room.

Eli was also concerned with "replacement." He asked if his grandmother would get a new husband and, pointing to my husband, said, "like you got a new wife." Over and over, he asked, "Who will say the prayers when we go there for *shabbat* (the sabbath), who will tell me stories of the old days, who will be my grandmother's husband? And is everyone else all right?"

I was unable to attend the funeral because it was the day of my youngest daughter's graduation from college, and although many family members offered to sit with Eli at the funeral and take him out if he felt that he didn't want to stay, his parents decided to let him visit a school friend for a few days and not attend the funeral. I'm sure it was easier for his mother not to have to worry about him, but I felt—and much of the literature supports this—that it would have been better for him to have been there. He was used to going to synagogue, so the religious aspects of the service would not have overwhelmed him. He could have actively participated with others in their expressions of grief and, indeed, he might have found it supportive to see how many people came to the service to honor his grandfather's memory. I think that Eli may feel later that he was deprived of the experience, and that his parents did not perceive the importance of this loss in his life. He is not a child who is often left with sitters when his parents go visiting, he is used to being included. This exclusion may seem unwarranted to him. However, his father did take Eli to the cemetery later and gave him a chance to say good-bye in his own way, and perhaps to come to terms with the finality of the death. His parents do plan to include Eli in the unveiling activities. And when Eli saw the Sesame Street segment about the death of Mr. Hooper, he told me that Big Bird was silly. "He should know you can't come alive again." Eli had clearly learned that his Sabah couldn't possibly come back.

Too often we think that children later forget their experiences with death. We are aware that the effects of losses remain and may have an impact on their ego development, but we often assume that much of the conscious material is forgotten. This just isn't so. My father, whose mother died when he was 12, would still get choked up 70 years later when he described the months preceding her death and the funeral itself. He could describe, almost in minute detail, the long horse-and-carriage ride to the cemetery and then the stop at a restaurant on the way back. He remembered not being able to eat anything, and wondering how anyone could eat, as if nothing had happened, when his mother had just been buried.

Last week, I received a letter from the retired headmistress of the high school from which I graduated 35 years ago. She knew I was speaking on this topic and shared her own experiences with me. These experiences date back to the early part of the century.

> In my case, I was brought up in my grandparents' home, and they lived on until I was in my twenties. But there was a great-grandmother who visited us, and I have no recollection of her death. She just wasn't there any more. The death of my father, when I was five, was a different matter. Even then, every effort was made to protect my sisters and me. Later I was told that whenever mother returned home she

took off her mandatory "widow's weeds" before letting
us see her. That was a brave effort and yet, for
years afterwards, my eyes would fill with tears when
I thought of him.

I'm certain that many could relate similar stories of the
first time they experienced the death of a significant adult.
Although the event occurred years ago, in many ways it still
seems like yesterday.
This past October, my stepdaughter's father-in-law died.
My stepdaughter has a son who was almost six at the time.
Ephram had just seen this grandfather at a wedding party in
California, at which time he appeared to have made a good
recovery from a heart attack. Ephram's comments were interesting. He said he was glad that they had taken pictures at
the wedding. He also said that it was good that his grandfather had had a heart attack earlier, because if he hadn't
his parents might not have taken him with them to California.
Ephram clearly felt that he had been given an opportunity to
say good-bye. He also alluded to the fact that after his grandfather's first attack, the family realized that he wasn't going
to live forever. Ephram said he was sad that they hadn't taken
movies, just stills, because now they couldn't see him move
anymore. Ephram wanted to keep this grandpa as alive as he
could.
Ephram was included in the funeral and *shiva*, and seemed
to find this helpful. A few of us took him to lunch after the
funeral (he did not go to the cemetery), and when he returned
home he helped to receive the guests. He understood that
many people cared about his family and that that was why
they visited. This very sad situation was, nevertheless, a
positive and warm experience for Ephram.
I have recognized a recurring theme among many medical
students who elect to take a course on death and dying. These
young people report that they had been unable to participate
with other mourners at the time of death of a close friend or
family member. Often they had not been told of the death by
their parents, who didn't want to interrupt college classes or
a well-earned summer vacation. They report that their individual mourning at a later day didn't have the significance it
would have had if they had shared it with others.
All of us who work or live with children are sometime
faced with the dilemma of "how to tell" or "how to cope," and
I suspect that if we simply remember how children perceive
death *and* life, and if we put the child's needs before our own
(or let someone else do it, if we just can't at that time), our
instincts will lead us to effective behavior. Sometimes, however,
in families for whom religion, any religion, plays an important
part, there is a tendency to speak of heaven, to tell children
that "God called" for those who have died, that they are "just
asleep," or that they are on a "special journey." All these

phrases can fill children with anxiety, and serve no purpose other than to make it temporarily easier for the adults.

Grief is hard work for all of us. Sometimes it is hardest for children, not only because of their vulnerability, but often because the people they most need to help them through the difficult period are experiencing grief themselves. At such a time they have available fewer emotional resources, or even fewer cognitive resources than usual.

When my father died last year, I worked through some of my own grief by making up a little book for my grandson that his parents could read to him later. Illustrated with photographs, it told the story of all the important people in my grandson's life: his parents, grandparents, two great-grandmothers, and his great-grandfather, Papa. The book ended with the following.

> Papa couldn't drive his car any more. He couldn't
> visit Matt anymore. Papa had died. "Died" means
> we can't ever see Papa any more. But we can re-
> member him. We can ask people to tell us more
> things about Papa. We can always love Papa.

When I dedicated my new book to my parents by saying "for many reasons, but mostly becaused I loved them," I wasn't sure about my grammar. Should I have put the love in the present or the past tense? You see, I may not always be able to accept the finality of death. How much harder it must be for a child.

REFERENCE

Fassler, J. 1971. *My Grandpa Died Today*. New York: Behavioral Publications.

15

Special Considerations for Research with the Elderly Widowed

Elizabeth J. Clark

In order to generate a framework for understanding the special problems of the elderly widowed, 39 women from the ages of 65 to 92 were intensively interviewed or were assisted in completing a questionnaire that covered demographic, social, psychological, and health factors (Clark 1984). This chapter will not focus on the research findings, but on the research process and the special considerations that researchers should be aware of when working with a population of elderly widows.

EXTENT OF THE PROBLEM

There are over 6 million older widows in this country. Fifty-two percent of all older women and, among those who reach age 75, nearly 75 percent, will be widowed (Butler and Lewis 1982). Despite their numbers, this population has not been carefully studied, and reports on the grief response of the elderly have been few and inconclusive. Several things may account for this. First, the elderly as a group are not particularly amenable to some of the standard research methods. For example, survey methodology may be a poor choice for this age group because older persons often have difficulty in completing lengthy questionnaires. They may have trouble writing because of arthritis. They may have difficulty reading the small print of many questionnaires. For some, lesser levels of education may contribute to a lack of understanding regarding the questions asked. Also, many of the elderly are fiercely private individuals and may not disclose personal information to an unknown researcher or by mail.

The use of qualitative methods, especially intensive interviewing, is recommended for use with the elderly (Connidis 1983). The goal of intensive interviewing is to construct records of action-in-process, and key features of such "conversations" are their length and diversity. Unhurried, free-flowing talk encourages the emergence of a wide range of

levels and topics (Lofland 1976). However, even with qualitative methods, there are special considerations that need to
be taken into account when conducting research on elderly
widows.

SELECTION OF A SAMPLE

Finding a sample of accessible elderly widows may be more
difficult than one realizes. As Sanders, Mauger, and Strong
(1979) have pointed out, obtaining participants for research
on bereavement is a delicate and arduous task, and it is almost impossible to have randomly selected normal ones who
are representative of the population at large. This difficulty
may be compounded when trying to locate bereaved persons
over the age of 65. It is exceptionally important to establish
credibility for your project and for yourself as a researcher.
Many people want to know the purpose of the research, and
"research for research's sake" may not be an acceptable reason for intrusion into a person's privacy. Many elderly people
are suspicious or frightened of strangers, and rightfully so.
You will probably need another professional or someone who
is known to an elderly widow (her physician, a visiting nurse,
or social worker) to vouch for you and to make the preliminary
arrangements. For example, when I planned to do some interviewing at a senior citizens' housing complex, I had the admin-
istrator suggest possible subjects and make the initial contact
for me. His reassurance was invaluable in my being accepted
by the women there.

TIMING

Consideration is particularly important when making
arrangements to interview elderly widows. It is useful to give
them several times when you could be available to talk with
them. It is also very important when working with the aged
not to appear too informal. For example, most older widows
are accustomed to being addressed by the title of "Mrs." Many
are offended by the use of their first name by a stranger,
and they may misinterpret "Ms." as "Miss." How well you
handle the initial contact will affect whether or not you are
granted the interview. If arrangements have been made by
phone, it is useful to send a follow-up note for confirmation.
It is also useful to give the women some identifying information about yourself so that they can recognize you when you
appear at their door.
Once the interview has been scheduled, be certain you
are on time. It is rude and inconsiderate to be late, and it
may cause undue worry for the woman who is to be interviewed. Another important point is to make certain you schedule

enough time for completion of the interview. A rule of thumb is to allow twice as much time for an interview with an elderly subject as you would for a younger one.

SOCIAL SENSITIVITY

Do not be surprised if many of the elderly consider your visit a social occasion. In my own research, I found that most of the women had arranged to serve some light refreshments. Many had baked a cake or some special treat. One woman served me tea by candlelight and used her best linens. The women mentioned frequently that they had few occasions to entertain any more, and treated me as a guest. It is important to accept this hospitality and not to attempt to rush the interview or the process. Therefore, extra time should be allocated.

Also, custom dictates that a thank-you note be sent after your visit. If you interview several women in the same housing complex, you should be aware that the notes will probably be compared. I do not suggest that the very same note be sent to each participant; each one should be personalized. However, I suggest that the notes be of comparable length and substance.

GUIDING THE INTERVIEW

With elderly widows, this process requires a certain amount of skill and dexterity. I found it next to impossible to maintain any set order. Research on reminiscence (Butler 1970, 1980; Merriam 1980) indicates that older people need to locate their present life within a larger biographical context. In accordance with this, many women told their stories in a chronological fashion, often beginning with the onset of their husband's illness or, in some cases, with their marriage. Some of them diverged and digressed with recollections that seemed to arise in unpredictable ways. These women needed to be gently kept on a flexible track. Others had prepared, in advance of the interview, materials they thought were relevant to the topics to be discussed. These included photo albums, journal entries, news clippings, cards, and other personal items. Unruh (1983) explained that mementos are objects that store recollections of the past in physical form and that stimulate thinking and guide reminiscences. All of the elderly widows had personal items on display, and almost every woman explained the importance of at least one of these objects.

It was necessary to allow for some lapses in memory, and occasionally some confusion was evident. Often the confusion centered around exact dates. Generally though, I was struck with how vivid the women's memories were and the attention they gave to detail. Perhaps as Unruh (1983) again explains, the sheer number of years lived, coupled with multiple losses

in old age, tend to make past experiences and memories a
central component of everyday life. For many of the women,
the death of their spouses had been the most traumatic and
significant event in their lives, and as such, their recall of
it was remarkable. One woman described the death of her oldest son in a swimming accident years before. She explained
having felt that nothing could ever be more painful or harder
for her to bear than her son's death, but that she had been
mistaken: her husband's death was much worse. Other women
told of struggles, deprivations, and losses, but felt that they
paled in comparison to the death of their husbands. Although
many of these events had taken place many years ago, and
time naturally would have dulled their impact somewhat, the
death of many of the women's husbands had also occurred several years ago (half of the sample's husbands had been dead
for ten years or more), yet that loss was clearly still vivid
in their memories.

   During the interview, it is important to speak clearly and
at a pace that is comfortable for the subject. Because of the
length and diversity of the interviews, I found it useful to
tape-record them. Doing so allowed me to engage more freely
in the conversation, and that tended to make the interview
appear less rigid and less formal. I used a small, unobtrusive
recorder, and obtained the subject's permission before beginning. I stressed the purpose of the recording and the fact
that it and all other data would be kept strictly confidential.
All of the women readily agreed to the recording process, and
several of them asked to listen to parts of the recording after-
ward. Many of them seemed pleased that their story was being
permanently recorded.

   During this research, I wrote a brief written interview
guide that helped me to structure the format and to be sure
that I had not missed any of the items. One word of caution:
because of the length of the interviews, transcription of the
tapes can be a lengthy and costly process. Also, it can become difficult to categorize such a mass of data. For example,
I had as many as forty pages of transcription for some of the
interviews. That amount of data can quickly become overwhelming when one is attempting to analyze it.

EMOTIONAL CONTENT

   Previous research has indicated that young and old widows
express grief differently. Parkes (1964) found that widows in
the older age groups showed less overt emotional disturbances
than younger widows. Ball (1976) found that young widows
were the most vulnerable group for a severe grief response.
Stern, Williams, and Prados (1969) found a striking paucity
of grief in their sample of widows aged 53 to 70, and Hyman
(1983) failed to find any severe social or psychological effects

of widowhood among his sample of widows aged 80 or over. These findings were not replicated in my study. Almost every woman in my sample cried at some point during the interview. This frequently happened when they were talking about the moment of their husband's death. Many of them stated that they had never before discussed various aspects of the death or their bereavement. When asked why this was, common responses were that "I didn't want to drive people away with my grief," or that "Everyone expected me to accept it." It became apparent that most of their grieving was done alone and in private. One remarkable woman read me poetry she had written in an attempt to cope with her loss. She called it her "Mourning Poetry," and said that she had never shared it with anyone before. Another woman told me a touching story of having received a flower arrangement from her husband almost a year after his death. He had been aware that he was dying and had made special arrangements to have the flowers and a handwritten note delivered to her on a day that had special meaning for them.

Other women expressed extreme sadness or anger at the treatment they had received from hospital personnel at the time of their husbands' death. Many of them were prevented from being present at the time of death, even though they had promised their husbands that they would not die alone. Others were not given the chance to say good-bye. Half of the women had been married more than 40 years, and felt that at the last moment they had failed their husbands. Many of them felt lingering guilt because they were not able to keep their husbands at home until death occurred. Some of them blamed themselves because they had not gotten help in time to save their husbands or because they had not realized how ill they were. Sometimes this guilt had been compounded by the careless remark of a physician or other health care professional who said something to the effect of, "Didn't you realize he was having a heart attack?" or "You should have called me sooner."

Loneliness was a problem for many of the elderly widows far into the postbereavement period, and some appeared to be experiencing a form of chronic grief. Yet, as they often mentioned, others see loneliness in the elderly as natural and expected and for that reason they try not to burden family and friends with their problems.

It is important that researchers be prepared for the emotional content of interviews with elderly widows, and that they be nonjudgmental, sensitive, and supportive. It is necessary to have a good grounding in grief literature and to understand the dynamics of the grief process before undertaking the interviews. Researchers need to be comfortable with the subjects, so that when emotional pain emerges they will not gloss it over, quickly attempt to shift the focus, or change the subject. Since the interviews require that the widows actively reconstruct the death of their spouses, recalling and reliving some painful memories, the interviewer has an obligation to help them deal with these feelings. The interview may be one of the first times that the widow has actualized the loss to another, talking about it and openly expressing feelings of guilt, anger, and pain. This is often therapeutic and cathartic for the widows, and must be handled with sensitivity."

SUMMARY

Little conclusive research has been done to attempt to understand the grief response of the elderly widow. Factors that contribute to this lack of research include the attitude that widowhood and grief are expected events for an elderly woman, and therefore are not a particularly important research problem; the fact that it is difficult to find a sample; the inability to use easier and more efficient research techniques, such as survey research; and the related problems that research with this population includes. It is suggested that intensive interviewing is a useful technique for the elderly population, but that special concerns of timing, social sensitivity, the guiding of the interview, and ways of dealing with the emotional content of the interview process need to be taken into consideration.

REFERENCES

Ball, J. 1976. "Widows' Grief. The Impact of Age and Mode of Death." *Omega* 7(4):307-334.

Butler, R. 1970. "Looking Forward to What? The Life Review, Legacy, and Excessive Identity Change." *American Behavioral Scientist* 14:121-128.

———. 1980. "The Life Review: An Unrecognized Bonanza." *International Journal of Aging and Human Development* 12:35-38.

Butler, R., and M. Lewis. 1982. *Aging and Mental Health*, 3rd ed. St. Louis: C. V. Mosby Co.

Clark, E. 1984. *Loneliness and the Interrelated Problems of the Elderly Widow*. Final, Separately Budgeted Research Report. Upper Montclair, NJ: Montclair State College.

Connidis, I. 1983. "Integrating Qualitative and Quantitative Methods in Survey Research: An Assessment." *Qualitative Sociology* 6(4):334-352.

Hyman, H. 1983. *Of Time and Widowhood*. Durham, NC: Duke University Press.

Lofland, J. 1976. *Doing Social Life*. New York: John Wiley.

Merriam, S. 1980. "The Concept and Function of Reminiscence: A Review of the Research." *Gerontologist* 20:604-608.

Parkes, C. 1964. "Effects of Bereavement on Physical and Mental Health. A Study of Medical Records of Widows." *British Medical Journal* 2:274-279.

Sanders, C., P. Mauger, and P. Strong. 1979. *A Manual for the Grief Experience Inventory*. Charlotte, NC: Unpublished manuscript.

Stern, K., G. Williams, and M. Prados. 1969. "Grief Reactions in Later Life." In H. Ruitenbeck, ed., *Death Interpretations*. New York: Dell.

Unruh, D. 1983. *Invisible Lives: Social Worlds of the Aged*. Beverly Hills, CA: Sage.

Part III

Interdisciplinary Approaches
to Bereavement

16

Understanding and Helping the Parents of Children with Cancer

Anneliese L. Sitarz

Despite the increasing number of people who are being cured of some forms of cancer, the word *cancer* still has a terrifying connotation. It is most devastating when the subject for whom the diagnosis is made is a child. In such a case, not only is there a threat to the child's life, but the parents and others close to the child invariably feel that they have failed the child in some way by not having prevented the disease from occurring. This feeling of guilt for having failed, intangible or irrational as it may be, is the greatest obstacle to some parents' attempts to cope with the diagnosis.

Parents usually ask such questions as, "What did we do wrong?" "How could this have happened? He (or she) has always been so healthy." "Would the prognosis have been better if we had come to you (the physician) sooner?" They may try to blame one another. Frequently, they will exhibit some form of anger. The anger may be overt toward the physicians and nurses who are caring for the child or it may be expressed indirectly. The near universality of this reaction in the parents of a child with cancer must be recognized. Unless the guilt feelings underlying the anger are understood, the anger will be misinterpreted and will lead to alienation of those in the best position to help. In this situation, therefore, physicians must try to make clear to parents that they understand why the parents are reacting as they are and that the object of their anger is the desperate situation in which they find themselves, not any individual. If physicians are able to do so, they will avoid the reactions of many inexperienced physicians who counter parents' anger with their own.

Most parents will be best able to deal with the diagnosis of cancer if they are helped to understand as much as possible about their child's condition. This understanding can rarely be achieved when the diagnosis is first given to them. The initial reaction of disbelief and shock can be so overpowering that the parents are unable to hear what is being said to them.

Physicians must recognize this fact and be prepared to come back at other times for further explanations.

HOW MUCH SHOULD PARENTS BE TOLD?

The information given to the parents should be as detailed as is commensurate with their educational level. Every effort should be made to ensure that they understand what is being said to them. When the parents do not speak English, an interpreter who can clearly explain what the physician is saying is essential. The explanation should include the manner in which the diagnosis has been established; the various treatment modalities that are available and their possible side effects; and a realistic appraisal of the probable course of the illness and the prognosis. A physician's impatience at this time will only increase the parents' feelings of inadequacy and their inability to comprehend. Conversely, the time the physician spends at the beginning to explain the disease process will pay dividends later in the parents' cooperation and acceptance of treatment. This cooperation and acceptance will, in turn, improve the child's chances of tolerating the disease and its treatment, since the child's level of anxiety is invariably influenced by the parents' attitudes.

Today, parents tend to be familiar with some aspects of cancer treatment through frequent exposure to the subject via the mass media. They can derive hope from the improved survival rate of cancer patients because of the increasing number of therapeutic agents and new ways of using them. Many have traveled some distance to a center that specializes in the care of cancer patients for consultation or confirmation of a suspected diagnosis. They may wonder if subsequent treatments can be carried out at a hospital closer to their home. Often, however, treatment at a local hospital is not in the best interests of the patient. Therefore, the physician should explain that because of the nature of the drugs used and their toxicities, as well as the need for supportive care in the form of blood and platelet transfusions, current therapy for leukemia and many solid tumors is best carried out at large treatment centers.

Parents should be fully informed of any research protocols that the child may be eligible to participate in. Most parents readily accept such participation if they have sufficient understanding of the therapy to be used and if they are assured that the child's well-being will continue to be the prime consideration. Such protocols usually require a signed statement from the parents indicating that they understand the treatment plan, the nature of the drugs to be used, and their possible side effects. The requirement of obtaining signatures helps to assure that sufficient explanations are given to the parents and brings them into more active participation in the care of their child.

WHAT SHOULD PARENTS TELL THEIR CHILD?

Once parents have come to grips with their child's diagnosis, they are plagued by what to tell the child about cancer. Unfortunately, there is no best reply. The physician should discuss with the parents the ramifications and implications of what the child already knows or should know. In this regard, the most important factor is the child's age.

Young Children

With a very young child (one to three years), only simple explanations of the immediate medical procedures should be given. In the case of a preschool child, age three to six, the parents must be helped to recognize that the child will become increasingly aware of the changes in his or her physical state, as well as of the parents' anxiety. Indeed, even if they try to hide their anxiety, the parents will communicate it to the child. Although the child will fear painful procedures, the child's main fear will be separation from the parents. Thus, the parents must be prepared to give the child some plausible explanation of the procedures, and especially of the hospitalizations. Children of this age can understand simple diagnostic terms such as "blood sickness," and should be informed of the probable need for long-term treatment and follow-up. Lying to them is deplorable. Even the youngest child shows concern, and is likely to express this concern nonverbally in the form of nightmares, withdrawal, or increased clinging to the parents. The parents' awareness of the implications of such behavior will help them to respond appropriately.

In sum, the most important way in which parents can help children in this age group (as well as older children) to cope with cancer is to keep open the channels of communication.

School-Age Children

Some parents strongly believe that even a school-age child should not be told the actual diagnosis, that the disease is incurable, or that the child may die. In their attempt to conceal this information, the parents may restrict all communications with the child. Yet, invariably, the child senses the severity of the illness and senses that information is being held back. Although, to protect both their parents and themselves, children may not talk about their thoughts or feelings, they may manifest their anxiety in other ways. For this reason, an adequate explanation of the disease processes and the need for continued treatment should be given, even if the disease is not identified by name.

If the disease is one like leukemia, which is known well enough by the general public to arouse strong emotions, there is something to be said for withholding the actual name of the disease from the child. Even if the name is not familiar to the child, its connotation to others can make it difficult for them to relate normally to the child. Some parents will use the word *leukemia*, but avoid calling it cancer.

Adolescents

Adolescents present a more difficult problem because of their exposure to biology courses in school, as well as to television broadcasts dealing with medical problems. It is likely that they will have heard about leukemia or other forms of cancer and that comparing the course of their disease and its treatment with what they have heard or read may lead them to the diagnosis. The resulting anxiety is likely to increase if they cannot discuss the facts with someone. Therefore, a frank discussion of the true diagnosis, the proposed therapy, and the most hopeful prognosis may lessen their fears. It may also help them to tolerate the side effects of some of the treatments, such as loss of hair from radiotherapy or chemotherapy and weight gain from steroid treatment. Adolescents are particularly concerned with their body image, so that they will be reluctant to accept, or may wholly reject anything, whether it is a disease or a therapy, that threatens to distort that image. The result will be anxiety, which can best be handled by honest, sympathetic explanations. Those who fear the worst may actually be relieved when the facts are given to them. It should be pointed out, however, that no information should be given without prior consultation between the physician and the parents. The parents' wishes about what their adolescent is to be told should be respected. At times, it may be necessary for the physician to urge the parents to change their thinking in this respect, but they should always be informed of what is being done and why.

Regardless of how much information the parents wish to give to their child, the most important point remains that they must be aware of the need of children of all ages to communicate freely about their illness. They must give frequent, understandable explanations to the children regarding recurring symptoms, the need for continued visits to the physician, and the need for treatments. The parents should encourage the child to ask questions and should answer as honestly as possible, keeping in mind the child's ability to comprehend, but never underestimating the child's anxiety.

WHAT ABOUT FRIENDS, RELATIVES, AND SIBLINGS?

In determining what information should be given to relatives and friends, parents must take into consideration what they will tell the ill child, since the relationship of the relatives and friends to the child will be affected by their emotional reactions to the illness. If the child is not to know the true nature of the disease, then there might be good reason to keep this information from most other people as well. In that case, parents might decide to tell the truth only to their clergy, the family physician, and one trusted relative so there will be someone with whom the parents can speak openly. Although this decision may help relatives and friends to react more normally with the child, it restricts the number of people with whom the parents can truly share their thoughts and feelings. Some parents find this limitation helpful. Others, however, have a strong need to share their problems with others and thus elicit the wide emotional support they need. Sometimes they can do so without the child being the wiser, but frequently the child then learns the diagnosis from a school friend or from some other source. The possibility of the child finding out should be evaluated realistically with the parents so they may act in the child's best interests. Sometimes it is useful for the physician to suggest that parents wait 24 hours after they have been told the diagnosis before they talk to many other people. They may then be better able to make a decision that will truly reflect their feelings than would be possible under the duress of the initial shock.

Siblings constitute a special category and must be considered separately. As with the patient, the ages of other children are an important determinant, but by no means the only one, in deciding what to tell them. For example, older children usually feel they should share fully any family information. Yet, some of them have expressed gratitude for not having been informed of the true nature of the afflicted child's illness early in its course because they feel that it would have interfered with their normal relationship with the sibling. Whether this explanation is true or is a form of denial must be left to conjecture.

It seems that family relationships will largely dictate what is said to whom. In those families in which openness has always been easy and natural, the parents will probably inform at least the older children of the sibling's diagnosis of cancer. At the least, the children should have enough information to be able to understand why the affected child is receiving so much attention and is the object of so much concern. Since they will sense the scope of the problem anyway, what they will imagine may be worse than the facts. Some children have expressed feelings of guilt, wondering if something they thought or did could have caused their sibling's worsening illness. Some fear that they, too, may become ill. Older children may be helped by speaking directly with the treating physician. This can give them a sense of participation in the situation that will help them to cope better with it. Twins of affected children merit special consideration. Twins often have been treated alike and have shared nearly everything. Serious illness or even disfigurement in one arouses especially strong feelings of anxiety in the other. This, too, must be explained to the parents.

THE INITIAL TREATMENT PERIOD

The first week or two after the child's diagnosis is a time when there should be frequent contact between the physician and the parents. As parents adjust to the reality of the situation, they have innumerable questions. They may request the same information repeatedly, and they may alter what they hear so that it is more acceptable emotionally. Much patience is required to help them accept the facts and recognize the meaning of their reactions. Physicians' and nurses' willingness to listen to the parents' doubts and fears and to respond to them sympathetically can do much to ameliorate the impact of the diagnosis. In addition, they can learn much about the family constellation and the child's place in it, which will help them give emotional support to the child during the illness. If the child is hospitalized, the opportunity for frequent contact is readily available and should be used. The child's hospitalization, and hence, absence from the home, may allow the parents more freedom to grieve. When diagnosis and early treatment are possible on an outpatient basis, allowance should be made for ample time during each visit. Although the separation enforced by hospitalization may be helpful during the early adjustment period, it may reinforce the parents' feelings of impending loss. In the hospital, as well as later, it is important that parents be allowed to participate as much as possible in the care of the child. Such participation decreases their feelings of helplessness. In addition, if the parents are emotionally able to witness procedures such as bone marrow aspirations, their presence at those times will be comforting to the child.

WHEN THE CHILD'S DISEASE IS IN REMISSION

Once a child's disease is initially under control, the family can often return to a semblance of normalcy. The duration of remission obviously varies for different types of cancer. When it is relatively long, the parents have a chance almost to forget about the problem for a while. Of course, the regular medical checkups are continuous reminders that the disease may recur.

Under these circumstances, it is difficult for parents not to single out the child for special attention or favors. Yet, it is important they not do so if the child is to be allowed to live as normal a life as possible. Normalcy for the child means being as much like his or her peers as possible. This does not mean that the child will not naturally have a special place in the family constellation by virtue of the need for frequent treatments and medical supervision. Some parents try to allay their feelings of inadequacy or guilt with respect to the child's illness by showering the child with gifts, trips, or favors. This special treatment is likely to evoke resentment in siblings and peers and thus disrupt the child's normal relationships with the other children. It is enough that the child feels "different" because of the need for varying degrees of medical supervision. This feeling, together with the possible side effects of the treatment, is bound to create anxiety and to stimulate the child's questions regarding the true nature of the illness, even when the child generally feels well.

The parents, as well as the physician, must see to it that these problems are openly acknowledged and discussed. Some parents are unable to do so. Then, when the child senses that the subject cannot be discusssed, he or she becomes even more anxious or withdrawn. A good student may begin to fail in school; an otherwise outgoing child no longer enjoys the company of friends. Some physicians think that when the child's disease is under control, the child may be better able to tolerate a discussion of the true nature of the disease than when the child is first diagnosed. Therefore, that is the time they choose to inform the child of the diagnosis. Parents may also find this time more acceptable in that they can honestly show the child that he or she will have ups and downs and can explain why treatments are likely to be needed for an indefinite time. An understanding of the chronicity of the disease, whether or not it is given its proper label, will make more tolerable the side effects of some of the treatments. In this regard, some parents find the analogy with diabetes useful, since in that disease as well, control is possible but cure is unlikely.

WHEN THE DISEASE RECURS

Parents always ask how they will first become aware of a recurrence of the cancer. The physician should explain as fully as possible which symptoms are likely and the probable treatment required. More important, however, the family should be reassured that the physician will observe the patient closely enough to be able to tell them if recurrence seems likely in order to minimize any delay in the renewal or alteration of treatment. The physician's reassurance will relieve the parents of the full responsibility for monitoring the child and will help allay some of their guilt feelings. It must be remembered that a relapse renews the threat to the child and thus reawakens the parents' feelings of helplessness or guilt. The parents' greatest fear is that there are no further modalities of effective treatment. The physician must be as encouraging as possible in this respect. If no effective treatment exists, the physician must assure the parents that the child will be kept as comfortable as possible and that they will have the physician's continued support—that they will not be abandoned. Follow-up visits must be scheduled even if no specific anti-cancer therapy is being given. At the least, these visits will convey the message that the physician cares about the child and allow the parents to raise any further questions and concerns.

Even parents who initially reject the idea that their child will be treated with new or little-known drugs—that the child will be treated as a "guinea pig"—ultimately may request that everything possible be tried. This is a time, too, when they may resort to "quack" therapy. The physician should try to discuss these unconventional forms of treatment to help the parents assess more realistically the possibility of success. The physician should try to prevent the parents from making elaborate expenditures for travel to distant places if, indeed, there is not much likelihood that the patient will be helped. In their desperation, parents have been known to go deeply into debt in a vain attempt to find a cure for their child. When there are other children, the parents must be helped to realize that these children must not be neglected, either financially or emotionally. It may be helpful to point out that when the patient dies, the other children can be a source of comfort. If, however, parents are then no longer able to provide adequately for them or if the children have developed serious problems as a result of emotional neglect, the grief can be compounded.

DURING THE TERMINAL ILLNESS

When a child becomes terminally ill or when there is no further treatment available, the family enters a new state of crisis. Parents who have been coping well while the child's disease was in remission may again become angry and difficult to manage. It has been found that parents who are best able to accept the diagnosis are usually also best able to cope with the fact that the illness is terminal. They can do so partly because the physician spent time explaining the disease process and their reactions to it from the time of the diagnosis. Those parents who have not received this kind of support will show the most anger as the situation becomes more desperate.

In addition to struggling to handle their own emotions, parents are once again faced with the question of what to tell the child. Regardless of how much they previously may have wanted to protect the child from knowing the true diagnosis, they are now faced with the reality that the child will die.

Even preschool children give evidence of a sense of impending doom. Often they become withdrawn, refusing to relate or speak to their parents. Their withdrawal is distressing to the parents, who feel they are not wanted and thus are even more helpless. It may help the parents to realize that although the young child's concept of death may not be the same as that of older people, the child is aware that something awesome is happening. The child's greatest fear is of being left alone. Thus, even if the child does not talk to the parents, the parents can be sure that their presence at the child's bedside has a comforting effect.

Older children may actually talk of dying. Adolescents may talk more fully of their feelings. In actual practice, however, most do not do so—at least not to their parents—often because they want to spare the parents further agony. Their failure to talk leads to a situation in which no meaningful communication between the parents and the child is possible, both wishing to avoid the subject uppermost in their thoughts. Sometimes the physician or a nurse can act as an intermediary; either the patient or the parents can discuss with the intermediary what is troubling them and the intermediary can transmit this information. In some situations, the rift is so great that this form of communication is the only one possible, but then it can relieve the tension and lessen the patient's feelings of isolation.

Once again, decisions must be made about what the siblings should be told and when the inevitability of the patient's death should be relayed to them. If death appears imminent, the siblings probably should be told immediately because they need time to adjust. Some siblings who were not informed of the possibility of death but were told only after the patient had died have been deeply resentful toward their parents for lying to them. More than anything, the members of the family need to support each other at this time. Therefore, their openness with one another is essential.

WHEN THE CHILD DIES

Once they have accepted the inevitability of death, most parents want to know exactly what to expect when the child dies. Even though it is not always possible to give them precise information, the physician must recognize that the parents need a lot of preparation and should allow sufficient time to give them emotional support. As before, the parents should be encouraged to help in the daily care of the patient. They should be allowed to be present at the bedside as much as they wish, especially when the child dies. Their presence at the final moment gives them the satisfaction of knowing that they were there if the child needed them or called for them and that everything possible was done to ease the child's pain and anxiety.

Incidentally, when parents are present at the time of death, it is easier to gain their permission to perform an autopsy. Whether parents should be asked to give such permission depends on the circumstances of the child's death and the interest of the staff of a teaching institution. The granting of permission for an autopsy should be considered a gift from the parents and the child that may help future children with similar problems. When it is considered in this light, the idea of an autopsy may be more acceptable to the parents. The physician can also assure parents who may have lingering doubts about some aspect of the illness that the examination may give more definitive information.

When the parents are not present at the child's death, the physician must make the difficult decision of whether to inform them of the child's death by telephone or to have them come to the hospital under the pretext of the child's "worsening condition." The former decision may interfere with the parents' relationship with the physician and the support the parents derive from it, while the latter decision can create the risk of an accidental injury to the parents in their rush to get to the hospital on time when, in fact, it is too late. Therefore, the physician must treat each case individually.

AFTER THE CHILD'S DEATH

Parents who have developed a warm relationship with the physician often find it helpful to keep in contact in some manner after the child's death. Since he or she was the last person to be involved with their child, they feel close to the physician. Thus, the physician can offer the parents the opportunity to call in two or three months if they wish to discuss the findings of the autopsy or if nagging questions remain. Such a suggestion allows the parents to make a choice but offers them a definite opportunity for further support. Some parents will not telephone because they are afraid of recalling painful memories. For others, emotional support may be needed after the child's death as much as it was before, to help them through the period of mourning.

SUMMARY

Much can be done to ease the devastating impact on parents of their child's diagnosis of cancer. The initial shock and disbelief must be overcome before parents are able to accept the reality of the diagnosis. This requires much patience and understanding from the staff. The parents are greatly concerned about how much the child will have to suffer, both physically and emotionally; and they should be given as much information as possible about the symptoms, likely treatment, and probable course of the disease. As outlined, the implications of the diagnosis for the child and the child's siblings, as well as for relatives and friends, should be considered. Parents should be encouraged to discuss their fears with the physician and should be certain of the physician's support through all phases of the illness and even after the child has died. The more the physician helps parents to understand the disease and their reactions to it, the more they, in turn, will be able to be supportive to the child.

17

The Nurse, the Terminally Ill, and Acute Grief

Carolyn Winget and
Marilyn C. Sholiton

These quotations from the literature on the care of the dying are so ubiquitous that they could be replicated quickly by anyone who is knowledgeable about this field.

> There do not seem to be norms regarding appropriate behavior toward a person whose death is considered inevitable. . . . Studies indicate that communication between dying patients and both staff and relatives is poor. (Crane 1970)

> Effective emotional support of dying persons by medical personnel apparently occurs relatively infrequently . . . medical personnel prefer to treat dying persons as if they were expected to live. (Duff and Hollingshead 1968)

> 'No matter what my personal beliefs, in my role as a medical professional I would fight to keep the patient alive.' Of nurses surveyed, almost half agreed with this statement; another one-fourth were undecided. Among physicians, the comparable figures were 33 percent and 17 percent. (Winget, Kapp, and Yeaworth 1977)

> Attitudes toward dying depend on whether the process occurs at the end or as a break in the life cycle. The second is subject to vigorous intervention and is not considered an appropriate death. (Parsons and Lidz 1967)

It is within the context of these typical traditional statements that we wish to look at the changing roles of nurses in the care of the terminally ill and in the management of acute grief. The changes in these roles have not evolved in a vacuum, but have been affected by new directions and broadly based philosophical, moral, and ethical discussions that today involve legal and medical professionals, the interested public, hospital systems, and, most recently, branches of the federal government. Crane (1970) referred to a lack of norms to guide appropriate behavior toward a dying person. Such norms now seem to be emerging and to be amenable to explication. In turn, these developing norms are having a profound influence on decisions about whether or not to prolong the dying process, on the closed or open context of interpersonal relations during terminal illness, and on the management of acute grief.

The following definition should guide our exploration. An acute grief reaction is characterized by feelings of sadness, loss of interest in the external world, loss of zest for life, a decrease in appetite and libido, disturbance of sleep patterns, and preoccupation with impending loss. Shock and disbelief are frequent initial responses, as are denial, despair, and irritability. The distinctive separation anxiety experienced during the typical acute grief reaction is associated with feelings of loss, loneliness, and emptiness. Depression in association with an acute grief reaction is often tinged with feelings of guilt. These feelings are experienced not only by patients who are mourning for the impending loss of life itself, but by their families, close friends, and health caregivers.

Using two case illustrations, this study focuses on the methods used on a hospital ward where the nurses have uniquely equipped themselves to cope with untimely death. Problems of interacting with dying patients are minimized, the impact of terminal illness on families is handled with sensitivity and sharing, patients' unfinished business is attended to, and continuity of care through the sharing of important information is a constant goal. The difficulties nurses face in providing this type of effective emotional support for dying patients, their families, and members of the health care team will be discussed. In the process of providing that support, the anonymity and alienation so often said to accompany death in a modern urban hospital are lessened, albeit not eliminated. Both of the patients whose cases will be presented were relatively young, and thus fit the concept of "untimely death" (Weisman 1973). Also, both patients received the news of their prognosis with stunned disbelief and an acute grief reaction; both died within relatively brief periods thereafter.

CASE NO. 1: MRS. K

Late in the summer of 1983, Mrs. K, a married 41-year-old woman who was the mother of three adult sons, appeared at the hospital emergency unit with complaints of abdominal pains. She was diagnosed as having gastroenteritis, treated, and discharged. One week later she was admitted to the hospital with the following symptoms: nausea for the previous ten days, considerable abdominal pain, blood-streaked vomiting immediately after eating, a 25-pound weight loss within four months, loose blood-streaked stools, and a history of constipation that had been chronic since the time of a hysterectomy 15 years earlier. Mrs. K died 20 days after her hospital admission.

During that period, she underwent medical procedures that included endoscopy, placement of a nasogastric tube for hyperalimentation, a subclavicular lymph node biopsy, a subtotal gastrectomy, and palliative chemotherapy. Dilaudid, morphine, nembutal, and Valium were all used at various times to control her pain and agitation. At a family conference held the day after the gastrectomy, Mrs. K's status and her poor prognosis were frankly discussed. There was massive denial of this information: Family members subsequently questioned the staff about how soon Mrs. K would be ready to return to work. Mrs. K talked about wanting to get well fast and return home because her family needed her. An offer of an additional conference at which the oncologist would answer their questions was refused by the patient.

As the nursing staff continued her physical care, they made it clear to Mrs. K that there were no "forbidden" topics for discussion. Mrs. K increasingly shared her fears, her hopes, her frustrations. Her three adult sons were the result of a previous, conflict-laden marriage. The oldest of the three was in prison; the second, "my good son," was in military service and briefly returned home on compassionate leave; the third son was unemployed and an alcoholic. Mrs. K felt strongly about his continuing need of her stabilizing influence.

Six weeks before entering the hospital, she had married Mr. K, a man with whom she had had a warm and sharing relationship for several years. His constant attendance at the hospital and his loving attention to his wife's needs strongly influenced the course of her terminal illness. The nursing staff felt that even before her hospital admission, perhaps even at the time of her marriage, Mrs. K had known, albeit at the preconscious level, that she was dying. Shifts from ambivalence, to denial, to reality-oriented depression about her status were frequent. Even while discussing "getting better and going home," she said "I don't know how much time I have left and I want to make the most of it." She also made overt and very clear statements about not wanting heroic measures performed to prolong her life. Her only request was that her medication be adequate to control pain. Mr. K, in contrast, wanted everything possible done for his wife. It was only for him that she agreed to the surgery and other painful procedures, especially the tube feeding and chemotherapy.

As she became more tired and weak, and as her abdomen and legs became increasingly swollen, Mrs. K relied more and more heavily on the nursing staff for support. She talked freely to them of her sadness and her fears of the unknown,

and of things she wanted to do before she died. One thing
she wanted deeply was to see her imprisoned son once more
to say good-bye. Unfortunately, in spite of the efforts initiated by the nurses and hospital staff, the prison was unable
to fulfill this request; as a compromise, the nursing staff
arranged for Mrs. K to talk to her son by long-distance
telephone.

Another request was more easily managed. Mrs. K was in
a room by herself, and she wanted a final time of privacy with
her husband. Five days prior to her death, when she was
having a brief period of feeling better, this was arranged.
During Mr. K's usual visit, the door was closed and a "crash
cart" placed in front of it to stop inadvertent intrusion.

A chart entry made by Mrs. K's surgeon on the day before
her death indicates that the physician had discussed her terminal condition with her at length. She had insisted that she
wanted to be able to leave the hospital, and therefore would
be willing to accept blood platelets and tube feedings.

Nursing notes written—on the same day in fact, within a
few hours after the surgeon's visit—give the customary docu-
mentation of Mrs. K's physical care, and then continue:
"Mrs. K states that she wants to die and that she wants to
donate her body to science. . . . She also says she would
kill herself if she had the means to do it." Again, the patient
asked that no measures be taken to prolong her life. On her
last night, Mrs. K was very anxious and agitated. She asked
her husband to leave and requested that her second son, who
was again in town on compassionate leave, postpone his visit
until the next morning. She had always said good-bye to her
primary nurse with the words, "I'll see you tomorrow." This
time Mrs. K said "I don't think I'll see you in the morning."
One or another of the nursing staff stayed by her side most
of the night.

She died at 6:15 the following morning. Because the do not
resuscitate (DNR) orders had not been countersigned within
the past 24 hours, resuscitation was attempted briefly, but
the physician ordered it stopped. At a conference to discuss
Mrs. K's treatment and death, the nursing staff agreed that
on a scale of 0 to 10, Mrs. K had undergone a "good" death,
at least an 8 or a 9.

CASE NO. 2: MR. S

Mr. S, a divorced man, age 33, was admitted to University
Hospital in mid-March. He complained of sharp, stabbing abdominal pains, intermittent vomiting, and a 40-pound weight
loss over a four-month period. He had been healthy until that
time, with no significant medical history of peptic ulcer or
other gastrointestinal problems, and no cardiac, pulmonary,
or other problems. His only major illness as an adult had been

a bout of mononucleosis 12 years earlier. He was taking no medication, and had never had surgery or an accident. He smoked half a pack of cigarettes a day and used alcohol only on rare social occasions.

A week after his admission, exploratory surgery revealed carcinoma of the liver with widespread metastases. No further operations or treatments were considered. During the week after his surgery, the nursing staff worked closely with Mr. S and his family. He was discharged home to his family for terminal care, but the nurses continued to provide support both by home visits and frequent telephone calls. He died at home six weeks after his admission, one month after his discharge from the hospital.

Mr. S was an unemployed steelworker who had been living at home with his parents since his divorce two years earlier. He was a high school graduate; his hobbies included studying art, reading, television, and camping. The rapid onset of his illness caused him to look older than his stated age, frail and thin, with sunken eyes. Despite Mr. S's underlying distrust and suspicion of young women following his traumatic divorce, he developed a deep trust in, and reliance on, the nursing staff. That trust became the foundation for an understanding that encompassed the patient, his family, his primary nurses, and auxiliary personnel.

From the beginning, both Mr. S and his family experienced intense grief. Nursing care plans and notes explicitly addressed these issues, as well as the physical issues such as Mr. S's poor nutrition, control of his nausea and vomiting, and management of his pain. Mr. S was found to be shy and quiet, and the staff quickly learned that he was most able to deal with his feelings in a dyadic situation. Anticipation of Mr. S's anxiety, the possibility of his premature dependency, and his acceptance of grief and the cancer diagnosis were all considered in the written nursing care plans. The patient's ambivalence about issues of dependence-independence and his need to remain in control of some aspects of his life were understood. Overt expressions of guilt and anger were noted, shared, and worked through. Given this level of care, both physical and psychological, Mr. S could verbalize his fear of being alone, his fear of having inadequate support if he went home to his family, and his need to spend time talking about superficial things—art, books, camping, and his other interests.

During Mr. S's final month at home, the nursing staff continued to provide support through daily telephone calls to the patient or his mother. On three occasions, nurses also made home visits. When Mr. S quietly died in his mother's arms, she picked up the telephone and called the hospital. She said, "Jim just died, but you didn't tell me what to do next." The nurses made arrangements for the usual routines that follow a death. The nurses' final judgment was that his death could be rated a 10, that is, a "good" death.

DISCUSSION

A person's life is like a novel. There is a beginning, a
theme, and many characters who act upon the person; there
is a climax, and an end. When we are reading a novel and
have gotten midway into the plot, then find that it suddenly
stops, we are unsatisfied. It is as if we have been left hanging in midair. There is a sense of incompleteness, and we are
frustrated.

When people die, as these two patients did, in the middle
of their projected life cycle, we are also left unsatisfied,
hanging in midair and frustrated by the unfairness of life.
These frustrations and the need to offer a satisfactory end
seem to allow this nursing staff to provide patients with a
chance to complete some unfinished tasks, to have their final
wishes fulfilled, to encompass much in a short time. They are
able to help patients and families arrive at a more satisfying
sense of completion. They expect the acute grief reaction
experienced by patients and their families when they confront
a fatal diagnosis.

What has not been clearly looked at is the acute grief reaction experienced by the members of a caring staff that has
become a sort of extended family for the patient. These staff
members are the ones who care for patients during the fatal
chapter of their lives, when they are going through the most
private and isolating of all of life's experiences, the time when
the person anticipates he will no longer exist.

In their changing role, nurses are no longer the hand-
maidens of physicians, balancing their scientific intellectualism.
Instead their role is shaped by a holistic appreciation of the
patient. Various trends aid nurses in this holistic appreciation.
One important trend is the increasingly open context of terminal illness. Although Mrs. K and Mr. S vacillated between
denial and acceptance, both of them talked explicitly about
their idiosyncratic fears of death. Both patients and their
families had been told by physicians, in the presence of the
nursing staff, that their prognoses were poor and that recovery was probably not possible.

Another trend is the increasing awareness that the stages
of death are discordant, not necessarily in easy harmony
either within individual patients or between the patients and
their significant others. Thus, the nursing staff was able to
note and be sympathetic to Mr. K's unrealistic demands that
everything possible be done to bring his wife to a point at
which she could return to her family and work; at the same
time, they accepted Mrs. K's increasing reliance on them to
control her pain, to share her sadness and fears, and to help
with her private last-minute agenda. In contrast, the nursing
staff was able to counter Mr. S's premature dependency and
to enable him to return home, and to provide the secondary

level of support that allowed his family to be his primary care-givers.

A third important factor is the increasingly sophisticated and humane management of physical pain by means of proper amounts and careful timing of medication. The message of Cicely Saunders and other innovators of the hospice movement has clearly been heeded.

The nursing staff of this unit has evolved a comprehensive approach. Their interactions go beyond administering medica-tion, checking intravenous lines, changing beds, or watching blood transfusions. The dying person is the tip of the iceberg, and represents a family, a job, a community, dreams, and a reservoir of hopes and wishes. The staff has smuggled in a favorite pet dog to see a patient. They have arranged for a husband and a wife to have a few hours of privacy. They have made themselves available at all times to the families of dying patients.

The nurses of this unit work as a team and are supportive of each other. There is a mandatory weekly meeting where coffee and cake are free, but the nurses have to stay to eat it, and have to talk about what is happening. There is another weekly meeting with two members of the Department of Psychi-atry Consultation-Liaison Service. At these meetings, any and all things are open to discussion. These nurses know each other's strengths, respect each other's weaknesses, and care-fully assign nurses to those patients with whom they will do their best nursing.

When young patients are dying, ones who are close in age to the nursing staff, it creates special psychological problems for the nurses. The defense of denial is removed, making the caregivers feel more vulnerable and more aware of mortality. At these times, caregivers often expect the patients to do too much self-care because they want so much for the patient to get better, to not die.

The nurses on this unit help the patients, their families, and each other. They do not need anyone's permission to go to a funeral because they realize that they too need to say good-bye to a patient who has been so intimately involved with them. They too need to have a finalization or conclusion to the relationship. The nurses have also learned to respect patients who tell them they won't survive, the woman who says "I don't think I'll see you in the morning."

Death is part of living. Birth comes with the automatic fact that there will be death. No one knows how, when, or where it will come, or whether it will be instantaneous or prolonged. None of us knows if a supportive family will be there or if we will be totally isolated. No one knows what is beyond death. What we do know is that easing patients from physical being to physical nonbeing can be accomplished with grace and dig-nity in the hands of nurses who are comprehensive in their appreciation of patients and their families. And when this task is in their hands, we can feel that the ending of the story will have somewhat less sting than if they had not been there.

Weisman (1973) has described the desired result of this process: "Suffering is at a low ebb, conflict is minimal, and behavior has been maintained on as high a level as is compatible with physical status. . . . The dying patient indicates that what he has already done corresponds to what he expected of himself, of the people who matter most, of those to whom he turned for relief . . . and of the World in general." The acute grief is resolved because in the sharing and giving, life is reaffirmed and found to be worthwhile.

REFERENCES

Crane, D. 1970. "Dying and Its Dilemmas as a Field of Research." In O. G. Brim et al., eds., *The Dying Patient.* New York: Russell Sage Foundation.

Duff, R. S., and A. B. Hollingshead. 1968. *Sickness and Society.* New York: Harper & Row.

Parsons, T., and V. Lidz. 1967. "Death in American Society." In E. Schneidman, ed., *Essay in Self-Destruction*, pp. 133-170. New York: Science House.

Weisman, A. D. 1973. "Coping with Untimely Death." *Psychiatry* 36 (Nov.): 366.

Winget, C., F. T. Kapp, and R. C. Yeaworth. 1977. "Attitudes Towards Euthanasia." *Journal of Medical Ethics* 3: 18-25.

18

The Introspective Terminal Adult Patient—From the Social Work Perspective

Fran Belluck and Abraham Lurie

Some young people live all of their lives with congenital, chronic, and progressive illnesses. They may have to accommodate their lives and daily routines to include taking large amounts of medication, managing their diets, using inhalation equipment, and doing postural drainage. They are inseparable from their illnesses even though they may be visibly indistinguishable from their peers for a significant fraction of their years. Chronically ill patients and their families inevitably develop individual ways of coping with the demands of disease. These may include denial, confrontation, and seemingly casual acceptance. Individuals' own coping patterns may also vary, depending on their age and personal development, the stability of their family and interpersonal relationships and environment, and the stage of the illness itself.

When illness advances to the point that it demands more medical and personal attention and simultaneously decreases their tolerance and energies, individuals may develop a new awareness of their mortality and a new definition of time. Anthony (1971) explored the interrelationships between the realization of death and the concept of time, and the consequential anxiety concerning the concept of finality. This chapter is concerned with young adult and adult patients who are aware of the invasive progression of their illness, of their preterminal and terminal status.

Many of these patients have sensitive thoughts, feelings, and experiences that they want to express and share. It seems that in many cases they feel constricted in expressing their thoughts to their parents and to their physicians or other caregivers for reasons inherent in their intimate and interdependent relationships. The risk of creating any change or imbalance in these vital and precious relationships is too threatening and too stressful to chance.

In the Cystic Fibrosis Center of Long Island Jewish-Hillside Medical Center, adult patients have frequently confided in the clinical social worker about their need to verbalize and to

149

question. They have real concerns and valid questions, which can arouse anxiety, create confusion and ambivalence, and foster anger.

Some of the questions are very concrete. For instance, a few patients have asked social workers if they know what death is like or how it feels. Is there any pain? One 20-year-old girl who had been hospitalized two to three times in each of the last three years said that she had never actually seen anyone die on her unit, and she wanted to know if we have a special place in the hospital where we put the patients who are dying. She may have been asking for some confirmation of her feeling that she was dying. At that time I interpreted her question as a request to know whether dying patients are isolated from the caregivers they know and placed with strangers. I reassured her that our patients are always admitted to the unit and staff that knows them well. Other patients have also asked who stays with the dying patient. Reed (1967) wrote that in our era of drugs, it is isolation, more than pain, that is likely to be what makes dying so unbearable.

Patients also ask questions that relate to their parents. Do their parents really understand what is happening to them? They ask this because it is not uncommon for parents to continue to convey hope and to speak of scientific discoveries that might come in time to offer help. Tom, age 34, told me a week before he died that he didn't think his parents knew what was happening, that he was not going to recover. He could not understand why. He was even a little angry that his mother kept telling him that new medicines are being discovered all the time, and that soon someone would find a cure for cystic fibrosis. He was very worried that his parents would suffer from the shock of his death if they were not prepared for it. He asked for help in discussing it with them. I reassured him later that they did know, but that they could not let him know they did because it was not in keeping with their parental role as they defined it. They felt that they would be letting him down. Shortly after our discussion, Tom's parents, in his presence, gave the social worker a small gift, saying that it would be something by which to remember him. This was how they let him know that they knew.

Patients often express sincere concern for their parents' emotional state and physical well-being. One patient talked about the look in her mother's eyes, another about the pain and hurt in his mother's face. They speculate about how their parents will handle the loss, who will look after them, and how they will fill the time that was so carefully geared and devoted to their own care. In our many discussions about friends who have died, questions are inevitably raised about how the friends' parents are doing. How are they managing? Some patients express feeling sorry for their parents. Some

feel the weight of being an only child and leaving their parents
bereft and alone.

Now that individuals who have cystic fibrosis have the
possibility of living into adulthood more often than they did
ten years ago, the frequency with which patients survive one
or both of their parents has increased. This can be inconceiv-
ably traumatic for whose who have an illness that fosters so
much dependency and closeness. We have seen the loss of a
parent increase patients' anxiety and fear regarding their vulnerability. That loss can also emphasize the debilitating feeling
of inadequacy associated with chronic and terminal illness,
thus rendering the child unable to support the surviving
parent.

Patients' utmost confidence in and reliance on the physician-
in-charge evokes real concern for the physicians' health and
welfare, as well as their measured acceptance of their right to
take vacation time and to participate in professional conferences
away from home. Some people have openly asserted their desire
to hang on and keep fighting so as not to let their doctors
down. They describe how hard particular doctors have worked
in their behalf. They would like to be able to please their doctors and thank them by doing better. They know that their
doctors' primary mission is to save their lives, or at least to
improve the quality of their lives. Some patients have tried
to imagine how their doctors emotionally handle the loss of
their contemporaries, and how hard it must be for them.

Patients also sometimes feel pressure to endure and to
continue trying to improve in order to measure up to the
expectations of other caregivers, including nurses, physio-
therapists, respiratory therapists, and others. Although the
effect of these expectations may be positive and constructive
for some patients, others may feel uncomfortably burdened by
the implication that their failing health is somehow related to
an attitude of capitulation. One young woman could not forgive
or understand several staff members who made her feel guilty
about her fears, her depression, and her resignation. There
is subtle pressure on patients to pretend to feel better and
to look toward the future. Sometimes this pressure is interpreted by preterminal patients to mean that they have a responsibility to enhance their caregivers' strength to go on
treating them. Patients revealed that they are tired of pretending. They "would like to smile and mean it." They would like
not to have to apologize for the ambivalence that sometimes
makes them feel that they will push until they must stop, and
sometimes makes them need to take time out. They would like
not to have to acquiesce to the dictum of life-affirming professionals described by Reed (1967).

Patients have also revealed, individually and in our groups,
their need for the space and time to mourn their friends who
have died from the same illness or another. If they have allowed

themselves to make these friendships, why should others deny them the right to normal grief by maintaining a conspiracy of silence and withholding the information that a friend has died? Most adults have sadly revealed their anger at professional caregivers for this, and expressed disbelief that their parents could have known that someone had died and not told them. With the considerate intention of protecting our patients from hurt and identification with the deceased, we sometimes unknowingly belittle the meaning of friendships they have made with each other. Belated discovery of a death may elicit anger, accompanied by feelings of exclusion and the loneliness of mourning alone. Had they known, the patients would have wanted to share in expressions of grief with their friends' families and others who knew them. Thereafter, they may sacrifice the quality of future friendships because of reluctance to make new relationships. In the desire to protect surviving patients, the staff of the medical center may unintentionally be giving them a message about the ease with which we detach ourselves from involvement with their lives and struggles, and go unaffectedly on to the next patient. On learning about a friend's death, a woman said in amazement that none of the nurses or doctors showed any emotion to her. She wondered how they could do that. She did not know that the staff members had had a long, private cry. She needed somehow to be included. Cystic fibrosis is a hereditary genetic disease that may affect more than one child in a family. When one sibling becomes sicker, the other often becomes more fragile, more sensitive to his or her own vulnerability, and more aware of caregivers' reactions and responses. At the same time, the staff members may experience the additional burden of being observed while trying to cope with their own feelings of grief, helplessness, and guilt.

One seriously ill young man, age 17, overtly regretted his withdrawal from his older sister, who had died from complications of cystic fibrosis four months before. He felt guilty that he had not helped her and had not been there for her. After her death, he was able to say that he knew she must have felt deserted by her friends, with no one to talk to about her own observations of the changes she was experiencing—weight loss, decreased strength, difficulty in breathing, and more frequent hospitalizations. He regretted that he would not have another chance to help his sister. However, the experience of acknowledging these feelings enabled him to express his concerns about himself, to understand his anger about his own deterioration, to redirect his academic and vocational energies into more realistic goals, and to accept his own guarded prognosis.

Most patients seem to know, in a compassionate way, that their families are unable to respond to their self-critical statements and realistic appraisals. The subject is changed when it is brought up. Patients are almost chastised for being upset.

Yet, the experience of clinical social workers indicates that some patients have to voice some thoughts. These thoughts range from "I am trying to stay out of the hospital for as long as I can" to "I am afraid to go to sleep sometimes"; from "I try to feel myself moving and breathing when I wake up" to "Things take longer to do"; from "I am losing so much time" to "What is happening to me?" and "Which friend of mine will I lose next?"

The role of the social worker as a member of the health care team working with terminally ill patients is multifaceted. Corwin (1967) has spoken of the guidelines provided by social workers in helping patients and families to face death. "These guidelines suggest," she wrote, "that fear of the unknown is more anxiety-provoking than facing the truth, that children are sensitive to subterfuge and denial, that they are aware of their parents' anguish, and that they respond positively to a forthright approach."

These guidelines do provide a frame of reference for the social worker's function within the context of a professional relationship that usually spans several years of a patient's chronic illness. This relationship often includes members of the patient's family as well. The social worker's role is based on an essential foundation of emotional support, which may then be expanded to respond to other humane needs. Sometimes it includes physical warmth and nearness: touching, holding, and companionship. Sometimes it requires the provision of concrete services and comforts to patients and their family members. Various arrangements, some very simple, may acknowledge and ease the anguish and pain of separation: insuring privacy for a family; providing access to a phone or calling family members; or arranging transportation, meals, and a place to sleep. Social workers may be able to facilitate the family's use of a homemaker or home health aide to ease family pressures between and during a patient's hospitalizations, or may be involved in arranging for the patient to receive physiotherapy or to have a hospital bed, oxygen, or inhalation equipment for home use.

The scope of social workers' role can put them in a position to represent the reality of the terminal process by their receptivity to acute questions and expressions. By letting patients know that they are aware of the subtleties and complexities inherent in the terminal process, social workers enable patients to reveal their concerns, and thereby deflect some of their anxieties. A patient becomes aware of a social worker's understanding through direct questioning in which the social worker asks questions like "What did your doctor tell you?" "What did you overhear?" "Have you been able to talk to your parents?" and so forth. Social workers can dignify and give credibility to patients' right to be heard, as described by Kübler-Ross (1969). They can be catalysts through whom sorrow, comfort, anger, and grief can be ventilated. They can help reduce the stress on parents who wish to be sure that their children have the opportunity to discuss their current situation. In addition to reassuring patients and families about their own accessibility, social workers can offer support and guidance to patients and families who may want help in talking to each other. They can also reassure those patients who want to know that they will still be available to their parents after they have died.

Social workers, then, are in the privileged position of providing a component of comprehensive care that is unfettered by the authority of life-saving medicine or by the emotional stresses of parent-child alliances. Not all terminally ill patients are inclined to describe their feelings and needs or to verbalize their thinking. However, social workers' relationships with patients guided by an understanding of their individual psychodynamic structure and potential for communication may enable them to create a climate that makes these sacred reflections speakable.

REFERENCES

Anthony, S. 1971. *The Discovery of Death in Childhood and After*. New York: Basic Books.

Corwin, R. 1967. "The Role of the Social Worker." *Physical Therapy* 48 (7):743-748.

Kübler-Ross, E. 1969. *On Death and Dying*. New York: Macmillan.

Reed, A. W. 1967. "Problems of Impending Death." *Physical Therapy* 48 (7):740-743.

19

As Dying, and, Behold, We Live

Carole Smith-Torres

This story is not unique in itself. Every parent who has lost an adult child to disease shares the same problems: lack of finances; isolation from the community, friends, and family; loneliness, anger, boredom, depression, fear, and rejection, just to name a few. This particular situation addresses the uniquely personal grief of a mother in response to the death of her adult son.

The son, 49 years old, had suffered and lived with head and neck cancer for five years. His death occurred in 1982. My personal encounter with Mr. H came in the final stages of his life. His mother called my office asking if I would visit her son at the Medical Center. Mrs. H was 69 years of age. She was a quiet, jolly woman who, in her middle years and as the result of a search for inner peace and truth, had come to realize her need of a personal understanding and relationship with God. Marriage to a man 24 years her senior had filled her youthful years with bitterness and unhappiness. Five children had been born, one of whom died at age 2. She raised these children on her own, as her husband chose to play only the roles of disciplinarian and taskmaster.

I have attempted to explore Mrs. H's life in the hope of perhaps revealing the many dimensions of a mother's grief. What makes Mrs. H so special was her willingness to share her thoughts and feelings.

One of the most difficult interviews to obtain is one with a mother who has lost a child. Before I met Mrs. H, I had interviewed a woman who suffered from pathological grief. I was unable to make my way through 15 minutes with her when the mother retired from the interview. She had already canceled several appointments. Because this woman had never dealt with her grief in a healthy way, the wounds were still open.

After my first interview with Mrs. H, most of the pieces of her son's personality fit into place. Knowing her son was close to death, Mrs. H wanted me primarily to discuss

155

spiritual issues with him. He himself had attended church all
of his growing years. Yet, embittered by years of abuse by
his father, a marriage that ended in divorce and separated
him from his own five children, and now near his death, suffering with a dread disease, it was not likely that he was
praising the Lord. He had blocked out the entire world (except his mother). This included medical staff. Reflecting his
anger and isolation, he remained in his cubicle in one of the
wards. Blocked off by drawn curtains, he hid himself. As I
entered his world of agony, I sensed his need to be accepted.
To look at him was an almost overwhelming experience. Most
of his neck and face had been removed or deformed by surgery
or the rotting away of flesh. My second awareness of his
anger came with seeing a cigarette hanging from his mouth.
He puffed until the tiny cubicle was filled with smoke. I
touched his hand. He did not flinch, but rather was surprised that I was not repulsed.

Touching says I'm not affected or impressed by your
physical person, rather by who you are as a person. We
spent a long time talking about the rotten deal he had gotten
in life and about how rotten he had been. I spoke of God's
forgiveness to those who reach out to Him, those willing to
change and accept God's plan for their lives. His eyes responded to the spiritual message. His hard exterior was
melting.

When one is face to face with death, spiritual issues become paramount. He said that he wished that he had dealt
with them long before his illness. Now he had the opportunity
to get right with God, and find peace in his death. I left
Mr. H with his thoughts, a Bible, and other reading matter.
Weeks went by and he was released into his mother's care as
an outpatient.

Our next encounter occurred when he was dying. In the
emergency room, he lay in a pool of his own blood, racked
with pain. He was conscious of my presence as I knelt beside
the bed. He was placed on his side, unable to see me unless
I was on my knees looking up at him. His eyes searched mine.
They spoke of a broken, lonely man who had known the worst
form of human rejection. Now he looked to the only answer
for any peace, God. We wept together, I caressed his hair,
held his hand, and expressed to him God's love in a tangible
way. In his brokenness he was ready to allow Jesus to make
him whole. I asked him if he was ready to let go of the hate
and bitterness that had filled his 49 years. As I read to him
portions of the Scriptures that speak of God's forgiveness
and promise of eternal life, he expressed a desire to be right
with God. I prayed a simple prayer of forgiveness and Mr. H
prayed with me. His eyes shone with assurance. Peace was
his to have and to hold for eternity. I left him to call his
mother, whose only prayer was that her son know the peace
of God before his death. He died only hours later.

This interview was given by Mrs. H, and in many ways it reveals the desire for the God we trust in to come alongside us during our deepest need.

Chaplain Torres: Describe briefly your feelings as you antici- pate our interview.

Mrs. H: I'm reliving my life. The day my son died keeps recurring.

C. T.: When you realized you were pregnant, what were some of your first thoughts?

Mrs. H: Both joy and depression. The joy seemed to be stolen from my having three children so close in age. I had no support at home and it was during the Depression. I had five babies in five years.

C. T.: What were some of your dreams for this child as it grew in you?

Mrs. H: In those days you had so little, you dared not dream outside your small world. I had none, really.

C. T.: Describe your delivery.

Mrs. H: I had all my children at home. I never saw a doctor. My sister-in-law was a nurse and helped out.

C. T.: Describe to me the joys your son brought as well as the difficult times.

Mrs. H: As an infant he was very good and passive. He developed a bad temper in early school years. He was not affectionate. During his teen years, it seemed as if his favorite pastime was fighting. Fist fights and boxing. He tried to show he was like his father, a tough guy. He dropped out of high school and never went into the service. He got married at 21 and had five children just like me. He worked as an elevator repairman. His marriage turned bad, his wife was an alcoholic. They split up before my son got sick. He wanted to reconcile, but his wife did not want to. He then came to live with me. I was very happy that he had come to live with me. I didn't like living alone. I enjoyed him being there. He lived with me for seven years. During this time he got cancer. He didn't socialize much. He was withdrawn and read a lot. We would talk but not anything very deep. It was a secure feeling having him there. He was really sick two years before he went to the doctor with swollen glands. This became too painful for him. He went to the Medical Center and was told he needed exploratory surgery. They found cancer and after a tracheotomy and several other operations he had to have chemotherapy and radiation. He didn't seem scared. I was with him when they told him there was nothing they could do and that he had only a year and a half to live. He thought he could beat it and didn't need help. His old tough self came out. I seemed to see through this mask; watching day by day ate away at me, little by little also. My heart ached as I remembered my 2 year old taken from me. It's as if your heart has cords to those that grow out of you. Death is an unwilling severing of those cords. The pain is intense. Watching your child die day by day is like painful surgery that goes on forever. That is, until you allow a scab to form. You can get hard or bitter or you can accept God's will as you give to Him the hurt, anger, fears, or whatever else you are feeling.

C. T.: After your son died, were you preoccupied with his image?

Mrs. H: For about two or three weeks I sensed his presence on the couch where he always sat.

C. T.: Did you feel any guilt related to the circumstances of your son's death?

Mrs. H: I wish I had stayed in the hospital with him during those final hours. The doctor told me to leave—I did and I'm sorry I did. I had some guilt about things I could have changed in the past.

C. T.: How about anger?

Mrs. H: I guess I had a lot of anger toward my husband. Even though he had died many years before, I guess I never really dealt with all the anger until my son died. I feel better that I did.

C. T. Were you able to function as well as you did before your son died?

Mrs. H: One month later I went to work. It was good to work. I did well. The nights were hard.

C. T.: Were you able to accept the reality of your loss?

Mrs. H: Not until I felt a peace from God even though I had tears; I felt a peace with my tears—I knew it was God's will for my son.

C. T.: How did you adjust to your son's absence?

Mrs. H: Working helped. I didn't sleep well in the early weeks. There was a void, not hearing his voice. There were constant reminders. It took time to accept truth.

C. T.: How did you withdraw emotionally from your son?

Mrs. H: I didn't want to draw away completely. I had to accept that he was not near, but I wanted to hold on to some previous memories.

C. T.: Were you able to reinvest your emotions in your other children?

Mrs. H: They do not live near here, so I haven't. That leaves a big void. I'm not able to do the things I physically did for my son. I do visit the elderly and give of my services at church. It takes only a small amount of the void away. But that is growing.

C. T.: How did you express feelings of anxiety, helplessness, sadness?

Mrs. H: I went out a lot, walked, 'til dark; I thought a lot.

C. T.: What was living without your son like right after he died?

Mrs. H: Empty, doubtful. I kept feeling sorry that my son's life didn't turn out better for him. I was fearful at night, I missed my companion.

C. T.: Do you think you took enough time to grieve?

Mrs. H: Yes, I do.

C. T.: What sort of support system did you rely on most?

Mrs. H: To be honest, the Lord. I believe He has brought me through. I have seen others fall apart at the loss of a child. I can understand their pain. But God alone has been my strength.

As dying, and, behold, we live.
(2 Cor. 6:9)

Part IV

Funeral Service Concepts
in Dealing with
Loss and Grief

20

Helping to Meet the Needs and Wants of the Bereaved: American Funeral Customs

Howard C. Raether

The American funeral director did not invent the funeral. It was a part of Colonial America before there were paid funeral functionaries. Criticism of funeral practices and costs was a concomitant development. As early as 1651, the General Assembly of the Province of Massachusetts passed legislation prohibiting extravaganzas, especially at funerals. The so-called extravaganzas did not involve a funeral functionary but rather gloves, rings, scarves, and the expenses that went with pre- and postfuneral gatherings, including but not limited to the liquor that was consumed. At one time there were fines for people who wore mourning clothing other than black hats, gloves, bonnets, ribbons, and fans. During the Colonial period and the early stages of American funeral undertaking, there were no functionaries *per se* but there were individuals who sold burial merchandise. And, most times clergy were involved.

Colonial customs in America sometimes consisted only of a funeral service and a few prayers spoken at the graveside. There were also funerals in churches that gave the clergy an opportunity to give a lengthy sermon that was often made available in printed form with a skull and crossbones printed on the paper. There were "walking" processions from the church to the graveyard, which was often on church property. There were also processions when there was a service at a home or at a meeting house. Usually horse-drawn vehicles were used for these. One custom was to remove the pall that covered the pulpit during the course of a funeral service and give it to the next of kin, much as the American flag that covers the casket during the service for a veteran is given to a surviving person. During Colonial times, with limited transportation, arrangements had to be made to house and feed those who came from any distance to pay their respects.

Early Americans viewed and buried their dead with ceremony, most times including a religious rite. There were few or no cremations. The funeral brought people together in the presence of the body to declare that a death had taken place and also to give testimony to a life that had been lived.

Today, the funeral still declares that a death has occurred and gives testimony to a life that has been lived. However, there are some deviations from early American customs. There are deviations also from customs that surfaced during the nineteenth century with the introduction of embalming, the storefront funeral establishment, and the houses that became funeral homes. Finally, there was the advent of the one-purpose building as a facility for the period of the funeral.

Throughout the history of American funeral directing, there have been customs that relate specifically to the death of a child. For many years children and infants constituted the most significant percentage of individuals who died. As a result, there were customs relating to the funeral for a child, including special rites and ceremonies and funeral merchandise and equipment such as hearses designed for children. During the late nineteenth century, these hearses were standard equipment for most funeral establishments.

The deaths of infants and children are becoming less commonplace, while the number of adult children predeceasing their parents and even grandparents is on the increase. Since the early 1970s, such deaths have gained special attention in relation to postdeath activities and to the problems that death brings to surviving parents and grandparents. Often a part of the problem is the alleged lack of reverence in the abbreviated funeral, no funeral, or an anonymous disposition with no place of remembrance for the surviving parent/grandparent.

Today there are immediate postdeath activities that seldom existed as little as a quarter of a century ago. As the 1960s began, alternates to the funeral and to forms of final disposition other than earth burial were not known in many sections of the country. That is not true today. As we look at the current postdeath activities and methods of final disposition, we find that for most Americans there is still a funeral that includes a public viewing with a public service and public committal. However, there are an increasing number of funerals that include a private viewing but a public funeral. There are funerals that are private both as to viewing and the funeral service. There are public and private memorial services that include no viewing. There are graveside services only, as well as postdeath activities that involve immediate burial or direct disposition of the body without any attendant rites or ceremonies. There are also body donations, which are only occasionally preceded by a funeral with the body present. Often the residue of donated bodies are disposed of by cremation or interment in a common grave. Often there are no rites or ceremonies in association with the final disposition of donated bodies.

In many of the postdeath activities held without the body present, cremation is the form of final disposition. Indications

are that during 1984 the bodies of at least 10 percent of those
who died in the United States were cremated. There are various forms of disposition of the cremated remains, including
earth interment, interment in a columbarium, or scattering
over land or water. Sometimes the disposition of those cremated remains is carried out without any rite or ceremony, in
an anonymous fashion, in the sense that there is neither a
mark to show where the disposition took place nor a spot to
return for remembering.

The absence of emotion and the minimal funeral activities
observed today among adult children are increasingly encouraged by certain sections of the population. This can be
latently dysfunctional, as young children or grandchildren who
witness an abbreviated postdeath ceremony are denied observation of emotion at the time of a parent's or grandparent's
death. This may lead to the conclusion that elderly people are
not consequential persons. That thought can be carried further when an adult child dies and the services for that child
are not the social ceremony that serves to bring together
members of a family as well as friends and representatives of
the larger community. These abbreviated, often nonpublic,
activities often fly in the face of what parents or grandparents
feel should take place.

In conclusion, some parents and grandparents question
the donation of an adult child's body for medical science purposes or even the donation of a major organ from the body
despite the good that both may achieve. Some parents and
grandparents resent and resist minimal postdeath activities
that have contemporary values to some but are dysfunctional to
them. They feel the changed way of doing things does not
allow feelings and emotions to be expressed for the enhance-
ment of the common humanity.

Many parents and grandparents feel that the funeral with
the body present is a step toward the resolution of grief that
should take the form of a level of care following the death of
an adult child. And some who want to make sure that there is
a funeral following their death are prearranging and sometimes
prefunding such a service.

Among the first steps following the death of an adult child
are the care of the body and the meeting of the needs and
wants of those who survive, including parents and grandparents.

21

Meeting the Needs and Wants
of the Bereaved:
The American
Funeral Practitioner

Glenn G. McMillen

In ancient Egypt, funeral functionaries embalmed and mummified the bodies of the dead. Embalmers belonged to the priestly class, since embalming was a religious ritual as well as a physical operation. This double function of embalming was not carried over into later Western funeral practices, even though certain other burial customs continue to have both physical and religious significance.

Turning from ancient history to the development of funeral practices in America, it is worth noting that most of the Colonial funeral practices were brought from Europe by those who immigrated to the United States. Except for a short time, members of the clergy have always been involved in postdeath activities. In fact, the American funeral has almost always involved rites and ceremonies, usually of a religious nature.

During the infancy of our nation, there were no functionaries who were paid to help meet the needs of others after a death had occurred. Nurses, who were almost always women, served as the functionaries at the time of a death. They did not practice embalming, but bathed and prepared the body for viewing and the funeral. It was only within the context of those activities that they had any involvement with the survivors. Later, cabinetmakers, cemetery sextons, and liverymen became functionaries by performing postdeath activities that were ancillary to their primary occupations. These individuals had separate and distinct functions, most of them related to the disposition of the body. They were seldom involved with survivors beyond the performance of their particular functions. Without exception, the income from their primary work far outweighed what they received from assisting with funerals.

During the nineteenth century, undertakers, the American counterpart of English underwriters, became part of the American funeral scene. By the middle of the century, and certainly by its end, this development resulted in a shift in the role of funeral functionaries. Although many funeral directors still worked in association with cabinetmakers, owners of livery stables, or cemetery sextons, they themselves were unhindered by an obligation to any other occupation. It was during this period that funeral functionaries began not only to care for the dead but to serve the living.

Very little embalming was done until the Civil War. It was then that embalming was introduced as a means of allowing those killed in battle to be returned home for burial. It was probably because of this development that licensing of funeral functionaries began. Issuance of the first licenses for embalmers was based on public health considerations. However, if embalmers did anything wrong in the practice of their work, there was no way that their licenses would be placed in jeopardy. At that time, few women, if any, were involved in the funeral service in any way that required licensing.

When developments had reached a point at which the existing license laws were insufficient to cover some activities of embalmers, laws were passed for the licensing of funeral directors. These laws dealt with practices other than embalming, such as the fiduciary relationships involved in the provision of funeral services. State laws licensing individuals to practice both aspects of the occupation were called "dual license laws." Subsequently, some single license laws were passed, although some of the qualifications for embalmers were similar to those for funeral directors.

From Colonial times through the early years of the twentieth century, the greatest number of deaths occurred among infants and children. Thus, regardless of the licenses they held, funeral functionaries were attuned to the special needs of those who survived the death of an infant or child. Because of the limited life expectancy at that time, it seldom happened that parents or grandparents were still living when one of their adult children died.

As we look at American funeral practitioners of the 1980s, we see a constantly changing picture. People are living longer, and when they do die the event does not produce the trauma that accompanied the deaths of parents and grandparents as recently as 25 years ago. The elderly are often segregated in retirement communities and nursing homes. Many say that this leads to a situation in which the aged are out of sight, out of mind. Out of mind means out of heart, and out of heart often results in limited grief and mourning among survivors of the elderly. Even though this undoubtedly hurts some people, especially grandchildren and sometimes even great-grandchildren, it is not a universal situation. However, it is a point that must be considered when talking about the death of adult children.

Today there is perhaps more emphasis than ever before on the recognition and resolution of grief following stillbirths and the deaths of young children and teenagers, as well as the deaths of young adults, defined as those who have reached

voting age. It must be noted, however, that if, for the purposes of discussion, adults are considered to be those age 25
or older, funeral service practitioners are now encountering
problems in relation to their deaths. When adult children are
survived by their parents, the parents often ask, "Why did
my child die? Why not me?" As a rule, the older the child,
the older the parents, and the more often we hear this said.

The responses of bereaved parents sometimes reflect hostility. This is especially true if the parents have been segregated into an extended care facility or if, as sometimes happens, they have been separated from the child at the child's
request. This also occurs, when children and their families
have lived at a distance from the parents and have come back
home or communicated only on special occasions. There is even
greater hostility after the death of a child who lived in the
same area as the parents but who scarcely ever visited them.
Often, this also means that the parents have been separated
from their grandchildren. In this situation, although the parents may grieve, their grieving is usually held in. They do
not express it as a negative reaction or voice their feelings
about the way that they have been treated. In a sad commen-
tary on contemporary America, a well-known clergyman has
said that one of the few times that families still come together
is for funerals, and he added that it is better to have them
together then than not at all.

Those of us in funeral service notice another type of hostility. There are many adult children, particularly those between the ages of 35 and 55, who have mixed or negative
feelings about the social and economic value of funerals. Some
of them, in arranging funeral services for parents, siblings,
or even nonrelatives, seek very little in the way of rites or
ceremonies. Sometimes they have made arrangements for the
events to follow their own death, and have specified that there
should be immediate burial or direct disposition of the body
without any rites or ceremonies. Some of these people do not
even want their death to be announced. Older people often do
not agree with minimal postdeath activities, feeling that they
are a denial of the death that has occurred. They attach importance to the body of one who loved and was loved in return
When an adult child dies and there is a minimal service or none
at all, parents often resent, if not resist it. This adds to the
pain of their loss unless, by then, they have survived so
many deaths that it is all rather meaningless to them.

For more than a quarter of a century, increasing numbers
of individuals have been planning or paying in advance for
their own funerals. Most often they do so out of a feeling that
they are helping those who will survive them. Sometimes they
do it to be sure that they will have the kind of funeral they
want. Survivors frequently follow the wishes of individuals
who have prearranged or prefunded their own funerals. Those
of us in funeral service know that although the survivors

respect these wishes, the kind of service specified is not the kind they would arrange if they were in a position to do so.

When I came on the scene as a funeral director approximately 20 years ago, my peers primarily provided immediate postdeath activities. Since then, the role of funeral practitioner has been expanded to include approval of the prearranging and prefunding of funerals. Most recently, funeral directors have started to provide services to the bereaved that continue long after the funeral. We make our facilities, our libraries, our printed materials, and our advice available to those who have suffered the loss of someone they love. By providing such services, we also become the catalyst for self-help groups One of the most traumatic losses, with the most telling aftermath, is parents' loss of a child. This is true regardless of the child's age, although there are unique features to the loss of an adult child. In my opinion, when parents and grandparents are deprived of the opportunity to begin the grief process by open and overt acts after the death of an adult child, they are justified in viewing this as an unwarranted disenfranchisement.

22

Life-Cycle Stages as They Relate to Acute Grief and Long-Term Versus Short-Term Needs

Sherry J. Hutchins

There are distinct patterns in grief reactions that vary according to the stage in the life cycle at which the loss occurs. The life-cycle stage and the sex of the survivor are determining factors in the levels of acute grief and in determination of long-term versus short-term needs. This chapter will attempt to profile and discern the pattern of reactions that are common to widowers in general, and to widows in their 20's and 30's, 40's and 50's, 60's and 70's, and to those who are 80 or older. Further, there will be a discussion of the death of children. Patterns emerge when one distinguishes the life-cycle stage of the deceased child, from birth to adulthood. The complexities of the loss vary greatly as we view them within the context of the life stage. Grandparents, in-laws, spouses, estranged spouses, and children may compound the grief process for one another and for surviving parent or parents.

My degree in psychology and sociology, more than 25 years as the wife of a small-town funeral director, attendance at countless local, state, and national seminars, and a five-year commitment to bereavement follow-up services via widowed-to-widowed programming, as well as participation in bereaved parent support and hospice, have contributed to this study.

WIDOW-WIDOWER

In 1979, our funeral home helped sponsor the Widowed-to-Widowed Mutual Support Program, which has been described in the 1983 National Funeral Directors Association publication advocating understanding. This program is a three-faceted approach that involves the training and coordination of outreach volunteers, small group discussion series for the newly bereaved, and a social activity group that meets monthly.

From a five-year perspective of in-depth involvement with widowed persons of all ages, I have observed that distinct patterns emerge that vary according to the life-cycle stage

171

at which loss occurs. The life-cycle stage and the sex of the survivor seem to be determining factors in the levels of grief and in long-term versus short-term needs.

The Twenties and Thirties

The new widow in her 20's or 30's has acute emotional and practical needs. Most often she is left with small children, house and car payments that must be met, and an immediate need for help in locating job market openings and child-care services, or if she has been previously employed, upgraded job opportunities.

The new widower in his 20's and 30's may be temporarily overwhelmed by the dual responsibilities of home and children versus career. In our experience, traveling sales managers, small farmers, and laborers who are subject to changes in work shifts are particularly vulnerable. In the long term, however, widows and widowers in this life-cycle stage tend to reintegrate with the mainstream and eventually remarry.

The Forties and Fifties

Those in this age range who are widowed may not experience the same initial level of acute distress as their younger counterparts, but in the long term their needs may be greater. In our experience, the widowed in this age group eventually welcome small group support and the opportunity to create new friendships. In this age range, it is less likely that widowed people, particularly the women, will remarry, so a new social network is important.

The Sixties and Seventies

The widow in her 60's and 70's has a legion of reasonably active, like-aged widowed persons to join. In contrast, the younger widows and widowers return to a coupled community where they are, to some extent, oddities. Further, widowers in their retirement years, unlike those in the pre-60 age group, generally have some financial security in the form of pensions, government supplements, and health care support.

The Eighties and Beyond

The widowed who are both disabled and elderly may have immediate need for sheltered living or home care services following the death of a spouse. In our outreach program, we offer resource listings for such available services. In the case of the widowed elderly, it is unlikely that they will have the energy to forge new directions for themselves. Although their families may keep them interested in life as a continuum, memories often serve as their chief source of enjoyment.

THE WIDOWER

The widower, at any age, is a statistical oddity, and most often his initial needs are acute. Perhaps the saying that "women mourn, men replace" has its roots in widowers' intense loneliness and the lack of previously established male friendships. Would the widower be less driven to hurriedly replace his loved one, housekeeper, cook, and best friend, if he had someone with whom he could share his grief and ease his loneliness?

In providing follow-up services for the newly widowed, my greatest concern has been for widowers. On the surface it might appear that they are cold and unfeeling, but in general I see them as lost and alone, strangers in their own houses, haunting restaurants, traveling without purpose, and desperate for companionship.

In recognition of the special needs of widowers, our funeral home's community services program sponsored a "Coffee and Conversation for Widowers." It was facilitated by a local minister who is particularly well-informed about the grief process. The men met in a side room of a restaurant, and this small group setting worked well. Gathered around a table, the widowers introduced themselves and were asked to give the name of their wives and to say how long they had been widowed. This was stimulus enough, and the conversation flowed for the remainder of the evening. A thank-you note from one widower made the effort worthwhile: "I think the meeting did every man there a big favor. I know it did me good to just talk and listen to others' problems."

Our outreach volunteers who are women are sometimes hesitant to write or call widowers, fearing that their efforts will be misconstrued. Widowers can become paranoid about any female attempts at contact, since some of them are deluged with unwanted social invitations. The dilemma is that a widower will often feel freer to ventilate his grief when talking with a woman, feeling that he must hide his hurt and loneliness from another man. As we implement our small group sessions for the newly bereaved we are attempting to find a meeting place where both widows and widowers can share their true feelings.

ACUTE GRIEF: THE DEATH OF A CHILD

In the fall of 1980, our funeral home's community services division sponsored a Bereaved Parent Conference that was intended to forge another line of communication between bereaved parents and caregiving professionals. We invited local funeral directors, doctors, nurses, social workers, ministers, and emergency medical technicians to hear "what hurts and what helps" in the traumatic aftermath of the death of a child. The results of that conference were not only increased communication among those attending, but a raised public consciousness of their continuing needs and the establishment of a local chapter of Compassionate Friends.

Early in our marriage, my husband and I experienced personal grief when our first baby died. Our healing was facilitated three years later when we adopted our family, but a heightened sensitivity to the needs of bereaved parents remained. In succeeding years, when faced with the death of a child, we tried to do everything humanly possible for the bereaved parents and the family during the time of crisis. Nevertheless, we knew it wasn't enough, and that the hurt went on and on. We needed an ongoing source for bereaved parent support.

Compassionate Friends is a mutual support organization offering friendship and understanding to bereaved parents as they work together toward positive resolution of grief. Because of our personal history, I am an active member of our local chapter, acting as a resource person, providing literature and audiovisual materials, and serving as an outreach volunteer when a baby dies.

We have watched families without the intervention and support of other bereaved parents build barriers within weeks after a child's funeral, preferring to be alone in their ultimate grief. Further, uneducated friends, customers, business associates, and even fellow church members often expect the family to have dealt with their grief and to be back to normal in a month or two. The long-term acute grief that accompanies the death of a child most often requires the support of self-help literature and the patience and understanding that only another bereaved parent can offer before a positive resolution can be reached.

When a Baby Dies

When a baby dies, there is often acute grief. A miscarriage experienced after months or years of trying to conceive can be devastating. And consider the loss and mixed emotions of parents who had delayed pregnancy until their middle 30's or later On the other hand, for a young woman who conceived unexpectedly, a miscarriage may be less traumatic unless the loss is complicated by guilt or fear for the future.

A baby that is carried to full term but then is stillborn or dies at birth or within weeks is a human being in whom parents, grandparents, and siblings have invested hopes and dreams for tomorrow. The surviving family will mourn the loss of the future.

When a Child Dies

In recent years, volumes have been written about the devastating grief that accompanies and follows the death of a child. It is acute grief that may continue in its intensity for years. Society seems to be coming to terms, one more time around, with "death as a part of life," but death out of sequence is still considered an unjust tragedy. In our medically enlightened era, babies, children, and young and middle-aged adults are not supposed to die. It is unthinkable that children might die before their parents and grandparents.

When a Young Adult Married Child Dies

Our work with bereaved parents has included contact with eight families who have experienced the death of a young adult child. Their efforts to resolve grief within the context of spouses, estranged spouses, in-laws, grandparents, and surviving children were justifiably complicated.

The Carters' 21-year-old son, Donny, married his young sweetheart in December. Marty had left her parents and lived with the Carters for a year prior to the marriage. Donny and his bride had just moved out of the family home into an apartment of their own, furnishing it with borrowed furniture and appliances from the senior Carters. One month later came the unexpected motorcycle accident.

Don was on life-support machines for weeks. His young wife was, of course, the next of kin, and therefore responsible for the medical decisions. Marty's estranged father reentered the scene and became her new source of security and authority. Mr. and Mrs. Carter were powerless in a hopeless situation. This situation contrasted sharply with their unquestioned parenting privileges a month earlier, when Don and Marty were unmarried and living under their parental roof.

When the doctors finally declared that Don was brain dead, Marty and her father chose a funeral home away from Don's hometown. Marty went back to live with her father, taking all of Don's family keepsakes with her, as well as the borrowed Carter family furniture. In the traumatic aftermath of the accident, the Carters not only lost their son, but their daughter-in-law as well. Today a year after their son's death, Mr. and Mrs. Carter are still valiantly trying to deal with their grief and frustrations.

Paul Johnson, at 22 years of age, was experiencing marital difficulties. He was living part-time in his parents' country home while his young wife, Carla, and their baby son remained

in their apartment. One night he returned to the apartment
to find his belongings sitting outside the door. Angry and
depressed, he drove to a friend's home. On his return, Paul's
car veered left of center and he was killed outright in a
head-on collision. Carla was in complete charge of the decision
making after the accident.

Paul's mother, Janet, was well aware of her son's marital
problems. Grief at the sudden loss of her son was compounded
by anger and frustration, two common denominators often present in the aftermath of the death of an adult married child.
Paul's father's fundamental religious belief declared "If you
sin, you will be punished." He and his parents felt that Paul
had sinned and that death was his punishment. Imagine Janet's
plight. Within her husband's family, she was not allowed to
grieve. Janet would be the first to say that the support of
Compassionate Friends saved her life. When Janet discovered
that she was legitimately experiencing the normal stages of
grief, it not only reclaimed her soul but the Johnsons' marriage, and gave her the courage to return to the land of the
living and help others.

Janet's mother, from whom she had the most familial support, had died recently. Hers had been a second marriage,
and her husband, two months later, was already planning to
marry again. His bride was to move into Janet's family home
and assume her mother's possessions. The emotions involved
far more than a loss of material possessions but, with marriage
and two remarriages, a complete loss of continuity.

GRANDPARENTS

Bereaved grandparents who grieve for their child and for
the loss of their grandchild suffer a dual burden. However,
they can be a burden themselves. Just as a husband and wife
grieve differently, and therefore complicate the process for
each other, so do the grandparents compound the efforts at
resolution. How do we cope with the emotions that follow when
a granddaughter, crossing the male barrier, doing a "man's
work" by driving heavy machinery, is killed in the process?
It is difficult enough for those one generation apart to accept
a woman in a man's role, let alone those who are two genera-
tions removed. When our worst fears are confirmed, whom do
we blame?

Changes in society are contributing to the complexity of
the grief process. Most of us are living longer. Five-generation
families are no longer uncommon, and four-generation families
are the rule. The death of a child at any age has a different
impact on each generation. The resulting familial interactions
make grief resolution more complicated. We have grown accustomed to living with divorce and subsequent remarriages, but
when a death occurs, the heartbreak sometimes strikes twice.

Alice and John Bennett had a 30-year-old daughter, Bonnie, who suffered from an aneurism that resulted in premature brain death. Bonnie had been divorced for three years and had custody of her two children. When illness struck, the Bennetts assumed the decision-making role, and after Bonnie's death they took her children to rear. The children's father expressed no interest in caring for them. Another two years have passed, and now the Bennetts' son-in-law has decided to take the children back with him to the West Coast, despite the fact that the children want to remain with their grandparents. The Bennetts feel as though they have suffered two deaths, first through the loss of their daughter and now through the separation from their grandchildren.

In conclusion, no one can sit in judgment on the levels of grief and determine who is suffering the most. Every story has its individual differences. However, the overview reveals distinct patterns that relate to life-cycle stages, the sex of survivors, and their coincidental short-term versus long-term needs. The perspective may be helpful as we caregiving professionals guide those who are suffering into healthy channels of resolution. Bereaved spouses, parents, siblings, and grandparents may never be the same, yet we hope that they will not only survive but grow in compassion, sensitivity, and awareness of the life that remains.

23

Finding Peace in Crises

T. Earl Yarborough

Once there was a man lost in the woods. For days and nights he wandered around in the deep woods and found that there were no roads leading out. One long and lonely night as he walked through the dark, he came upon a monastery. He knocked at the door. A monk came, and before opening the door he called out and asked the man what he wanted. The lonely, lost man didn't answer the monk. Again the monk asked him, "What do you want?" Finally the man said, "All I want is peace."

Peace is what we are all searching for most of the time. Even the monk, who in this story was the helper, was looking for peace. The monk could never have found peace had he refused to open the door to this lonely, lost man. We are all, at some time in our lives, standing and knocking at the door of the monastery, crying out for peace.

Those of us who call ourselves the helpers of mankind—the caring and helping professionals—must be prepared to open the door for the hurting, helpless person, and to help this person find peace. If the door is not opened, we will never help anyone else or find peace ourselves.

I see too many people today in the human services field who do not care, or who do not want to be servants of mankind. They are so frustrated and concerned about themselves that they can't see the opportunities to become sincere givers of peace and to share their professional expertise with others. There is no way that these people can or will find peace for themselves. Until all of us learn the true meaning of giving, we ourselves are helpless people, not helpers.

For the past few weeks, I have been spending a lot of time in two different hospitals with two different members of my family. I have sat and watched the doctors and nurses come and go. It is a very easy, simple thing to detect the doctors and nurses who are givers of peace. The real ones tell you the truth, even though it is bad news. But they give you more—they give you love . . . peace, because they care.

Just a few nights ago, I saw a nurse enter the patient's room, fix the covers on the bed, and tuck her in for the night. Then, leaning over and kissing her patient on the forehead, she said, "I want you to sleep in peace tonight." As the nurse left the room, the patient went to sleep immediately, with a smile on her face. I saw in this nurse an angel dressed in white. I will never forget her because she knew how to give away love and peace. Her action might seem to have been a display of sentimentality. I believe it was recognition of a need of that particular patient by a nurse who was not afraid to meet the need in a very kind way.

If you're going to give peace to a hurting person, you must go beyond professionalism. When you made the decision to enter your caring and helping field of service, your life was put on center stage, where the light is so bright. Your sincere sensitivity to the needs of others—or your lack of it— will be detected immediately. A perfect example of this is a true story that happened to a funeral director recently.

This funeral director had just gotten home after a long, hard day, and wanted so much to relax and enjoy the warm comfort of his home. But the telephone rang, and his services were needed. He got in his car and drove to see a family in which the wife, the mother of three children, had died. As he parked his car, he saw a little boy about ten years old standing on the porch as if waiting to see him. The little fellow walked out to the car and said, "Mister, are you the funeral director?" The man told him he was, and then introduced himself to the boy. Then the little boy said, "You know my mother is dead, and I don't think I will be able to sleep very well tonight."

The boy took the funeral director into the house to see his father and two sisters. As they sat down, the little boy pulled a stool right up in front of the funeral director and didn't take his eyes off of him all the time he was there. Sensing the hurt of this little boy, the funeral director paid a lot of attention to him and made sure that he had a part in the conversation. After the conference was over, the little boy told his father that he would walk with the funeral director back to his car. When they reached the car, the little fellow looked up at the funeral director and said, "Mister, my mother is at your place, isn't she?" Of course, the answer was yes. Then the youngster said, "Well, you seem to know how sad I am because my mother is dead, and you seem to be such a nice man. So now that I know you, I think I will be able to sleep tonight."

You may be sure that this funeral director had a hard time driving back to his office because he was really hurting. He was hurting because he was not afraid to be human, to share his love, and to show that he cared about how people felt. He gave this little boy peace, and he received peace himself.

Maybe the following story will make the point even more real. A man died in the hospital, and his wife went from the hospital to see her funeral director. She informed the funeral director that her minister and some close friends had convinced her that there was no need for a funeral service and that all she wanted from the funeral director was to have the body cremated. The funeral director fulfilled her request.

A few weeks later, the widow and her daughter came back to see the funeral director with an unusual request. They asked him to please let them go through the process of planning a funeral service as if the husband and father had just died. The funeral director recognized their needs and took them through the complete process of planning the funeral. They talked about music, flowers, and all the other important parts of the funeral.

They then asked to be taken to see the caskets, and as they looked, both the widow and her daughter began to cry. The funeral director left the room to give them the privacy they needed. After they returned from the selection room, the wife told the funeral director about the game they had been playing of pretending that her husband had not died.

> We finally learned that we could only play the pretend-
> ing game for a short time, and the only way we knew
> to face the reality of his death was to come and plan
> his funeral. We know that going through his funeral
> at the time of his death would have been hard for us,
> but at least we would have had some support from our
> friends. It has been so hard for us to suffer all alone.
> It would have been so much better for us to have had
> a funeral service where we could have heard the beau-
> tiful music, seen the flowers, heard the minister, and
> had the comfort of our friends, who would have come
> because they cared. More than anything, it would
> have provided an opportunity for us to start working
> through our grief and accept the fact that he had
> died. It seems that at the time of my husband's death,
> everyone was listening to my words, but no one was
> really hearing the loud screams from my heart.

Anyone can listen to others talk about their feelings. Most of us are taught to be good listeners. However, few of us are taught to recognize and react in a useful way to the great needs, such as the one this woman had. I can understand and forgive her friends for not recognizing her true needs. But I find such insensitivity hard to accept in anyone in a caring field of service. The reason I know how hard this is to accept is that I am the funeral director who failed to hear this lady's "loud screams that came from her heart."

A dear family that I love very much had a son who was killed in an accident. Some weeks later, the mother of the

son gave me these words, which tell me many things about
how she feels and some of her needs: how much she loved
her son, how much she is hurting, and how much she was
looking for peace.

Silent Screams

There are screams inside me
    . . . so far, they are silent
    . . . there is no place to scream

I wonder how many other people
are screaming silently

The Jews had a wailing wall
Now I know why
    . . . Is it still there?

But Jerusalem is so far away
Is there a wailing wall anywhere in Charlotte?

I commend anyone who selects a field of service in which
the opportunities to give peace are totally unlimited. They
have seen and will continue to see a lot of deep hurt, and if
they are not afraid to be human, they will hurt also. Unless
they are willing to give a part of themselves to each person
they serve, they will look back at the end of their career
with a feeling of having cheated themselves and those they
have served. I do feel that the greatest personal satisfaction
to be derived from your field of service is knowing that you
sincerely care about the feelings and concerns of the people
you are serving, and that you care enough to share in their
hurt. We must learn to give a part of ourselves so that we
can regrow that part in order to give it away again. This is
a hard lesson to learn, and each of us will continue to struggle
with it forever,
Since April 20, 1945, I have been in the field of funeral
service. I do not know how many individuals or families I
have been with as they faced the crisis of the death of loved
ones. No two individuals have been alike, no two families the
same. Perhaps people are becoming more knowledgeable about
grief and its different stages as a result of the recent surge
of public interest in death, dying, and grief. But knowing
about grief does not make the hurt easier, although it can
help people recognize what they are experiencing at different
stages. There is no way I know of to avoid hurt and grief,
but we can give our presence, our reassurance, our concern,
and our professional expertise at a time when the need is so
great. Finding the point at which we can give concern without losing the ability to help objectively and professionally is
a goal worth pursuing. We must give both if we are to be of
real help.

If I could give a suggestion about how to give and receive peace, it would be that everyone take to their field of service an understanding and sympathetic heart. Then they will recognize and feel the pain of all those they serve. No matter how those people look to the world around them, *you* will see them as individuals who need all the sympathy and charity and helpfulness that can pour out from an understanding heart, as well as the best professional skills and knowledge.

If you take with you this attitude and philosophy, I assure you that when you reach the end of your career and have served your last hurting human being, you will look back over your life of service to mankind with great pride. You will have no regrets. You will be a contented person with a peaceful heart and mind. If you are a sensitive and caring person, you will not be afraid to be human. After all, isn't this what real life and living are all about?

Each of us should go out into the world in peace, have courage, hold on to what is good, strengthen the fainthearted, support the weak, help the suffering, and give love. Our gift to mankind will be peace for us all. The lost, hurting stranger is still knocking at the door of our monasteries. All he wants is peace. *You* may be the only one who can help him find it. Will you open the door for him?

Index

About the Contributors

I. Adler, Ph.D., Hebrew University, Jerusalem, Israel.

Fran Belluck, M.S.W., A.C.S.W., Department of Social Work Services, Long Island Jewish-Hillside Medical Center, New Hyde Park, NY.

G. A. H. Benjamin, M.A., J.D., psychology intern, Department of Psychiatry and Behavioral Sciences, University of Washington, Seattle, WA.

Daniel J. Cherico, Ph.D., M.P.H., coordinator, Department of Public Administration, Long Island University—Rockland Campus, Sparkhill, NY.

Elizabeth J. Clark, A.C.S.W., Ph.D., assistant professor, Department of Health Professions, Montclair State College, Upper Montclair, NJ.

Richard M. Cohen, Ph.D., director, Lexington Center for Mental Health Services, Jackson Heights, NY.

Kenneth J. Doka, Ph.D., associate professor, Graduate Gerontology Program, College of New Rochelle, New Rochelle, NY.

Mahlon S. Hale, M.D., director of psychiatric consultation services and associate professor of psychiatry, University of Connecticut Health Sciences, Farmington, CT.

Joseph A. Healy, executive director, THEOS, Inc., Pittsburgh, PA.

William V. Hocker, funeral service director, Grants Mortuary, Grants, NM.

Sherry J. Hutchins, community service director, Berhalter-Hutchins-Hutchins-Williams Funeral Homes, Kendallville, IN.

Frances Karlan, D.D.S., School of Dental and Oral Surgery, Columbia University, New York, NY.

Eric C. Keyser, vice-president, Keyser Funeral Services, Inc., Kingston, NY.

Austin H. Kutscher, president, The Foundation of Thanatology, New York, NY; professor of dentistry (in psychiatry), Department of Psychiatry, College of Physicians and Surgeons, Columbia University, New York, NY.

I. Levav, M.D., School of Public Health and Community Medicine, Hadassah Medical School, Jerusalem, Israel.

M. Lubner, B.A., Psychiatric and Epidemiology Training Program, Columbia University, New York, NY.

Abraham Lurie, Ph.D., formerly director, Department of Social Work Services, Long Island Jewish-Hillside Medical Center, New Hyde Park, NY.

Eric R. Marcus, M.D., assistant clinical professor of psychiatry, College of Physicians and Surgeons, Columbia University, New York, NY.

Otto S. Margolis, Ph.D., vice-president for academic affairs, American Academy McAllister Institute of Funeral Service, New York, NY.

Glenn G. McMillen, president, National Funeral Directors Association; vice-president, Fred F. Groff, Inc. Funeral Home, Lancaster, PA.

Vanderlyn R. Pine, Ph.D., professor of sociology, State University of New York at New Paltz, NY.

Howard C. Raether, J.D., formerly executive director, National Funeral Directors Association; consultant to National Funeral Directors Association, Milwaukee, WI.

David E. Sanders, Ph.D., clinical psychology, Philadelphia, PA.

Irene B. Seeland, M.D., assistant clinical professor of psychiatry, New York University Medical Center; attending psychiatrist, Goldwater Memorial Hospital, New York, NY.

Stephen B. Shanfield, M.D., professor of psychiatry, Department of Psychiatry, University of Texas Health Science Center at San Antonio, San Antonio, TX.

Marilyn C. Sholiton, M.D., associate professor of psychiatry, Department of Psychiatry, University of Cincinnati College of Medicine, Cincinnati, OH.

Mary-Ellen Siegel, M.S.W., A.C.S.W., senior teaching associate, Department of Community Medicine (Social Work), Mount Sinai School of Medicine, New York, NY.

Anneliese L. Sitarz, M.D., professor of clinical pediatrics, College of Physicians and Surgeons, Columbia University, New York, NY.

Edie J. Smith, program specialist, Widowed Persons Services (AARP), Washington, DC.

Chaplain Carole E. Smith-Torres, pastoral associate, Department of Pastoral Care, The Presbyterian Hospital in the City of New York; Conservative Baptist Mission Society, Staten Island, NY.

Robert G. Stevenson, Ed.D., coordinator, Columbia University Seminar on Death and Dying; Instructor of Death Education Programs of Riverdell Regional School, Fairleigh Dickinson University, and Bergen Community College, NJ.

Barbara J. Swain, M.A., graduate student, Department of Psychology, University of Arizona Health Science Center, Tucson, AZ.

Constance Weiskopf, R.N., nurse clinician, liaison nurse, Department of Psychiatry, University of Connecticut Health Sciences Center, Farmington, CT.

Ruth P. Williams, M.S.S.W., M.Div., D.Min., vice-president and funeral director, Unity Funeral Parlors, Inc., Chicago, IL.

Carolyn Winget, M.A., associate professor of psychiatry, College of Medicine, University of Cincinnati, Cincinnati, OH.

T. Earl Yarborough, funeral service, vice-president, Harry & Bryant Co., Charlotte, NC.